Praise for *Freedom Is Costly, But Priceless*

In *Freedom Is Costly, But Priceless*, Dave Meyer identifies what each of us can do right now to save the nation. We have abandoned so many sound principles—not because we've forgotten our history, but rather because so many people today don't even know our history. Dave shows us that America was founded as a covenant nation under God. This means that both we and God have separate roles to play. Dave identifies the simple steps we each must take in order to renew and restore that covenant. This book is for right now!

DAVID BARTON
Founder of WallBuilders

In this brilliant book, *Freedom Is Costly, But Priceless*, Dave Meyer lays out godly principles that must be in place for true freedom to flourish. The book is written by a man who has studied, observed and spoken to thousands who share this core passion. Without a doubt, Dave Meyer is uniquely qualified to address this timely subject of such great importance. In a world that desires to live in freedom, this visionary book is a must read.

TOMMY BARNETT
Senior Pastor, Dream City Church, Phoenix, AZ
Co-founder of the Los Angeles Dream Center

This book by Dave Meyer is so needed, inspired and noble in purpose. It opens hearts to the work of a gracious and merciful God in the gift of liberty to American Christians. We can find much wrong in a world that threatens the things most precious to us—family, children, faith, property and liberty. We are now called to reclaim and restore the purpose God gave America so many years ago during the founding of our civil government upon biblical truth and principles.

We sense an awakening and a new resolve in the many restorative efforts across the land, and we rejoice that today the American spirit is as able as it was with Washington, John Paul Jones, and Patrick Henry. But we must also learn that the root of the word *restore* is "story," and the prefix *re-* means "return." Restoration begins by returning to "His story" of America, and then by teaching it faithfully to our children for our children's children. As Dave Meyer exhorts us, "Christians, build your relationship with America."

CAROLE ADAMS
President of the Foundation
for American Christian Education

Jesus told us that knowing the Truth will set us free. That's a powerful spiritual truth but it has a clear application in our lives as citizens. David Meyer lays out the truth about our nation—its godly founding and the forces that are intent on destroying that foundation. Knowing the truth about our country will encourage you to love our nation all the more and spur you to act to do your part to restore our constitutional freedoms.

MICHAEL FARRIS
President and CEO
Alliance Defending Freedom

Dave Meyer is a godly patriot. As Dave and I were eating lunch, he shared some of the truths you will find in this book. In that moment, I felt a strong impression from God to encourage him to put to paper those things God was revealing to him, as I believed it would encourage and embolden many believers. Consistent with the humility and nature of a man who has done so much for so many without the noticing eyes of others, he was reluctant. Yet, God persisted, so I continued to urge him. Sometimes God uses a reluctant spokesperson, like He did Moses; they don't get in the way of what He is wanting to say—they just repeat His words.

I am honored to endorse this book and I encourage you to read it, act on it, and pass it to others. I believe it will have an impact far greater and longer than any of us can foresee. I am delighted Dave obeyed God's prompting. I pray this book blesses you along with the Body of Christ across America.

JOHN GRAVES
CEO of Vision America

While describing the people of Israel, Hosea 4:6 is also a perfect description of America today: *My people are destroyed for lack of knowledge* (NKJV). My good friend Dave Meyer compellingly makes that case in his new book, *Freedom Is Costly, But Priceless.*

As prophetic as it is patriotic, I encourage engaged believers to read his take on how we have entered into the mess we are in, but also his prescription for the way out. Dave is right: "Freedom is not an American idea. It's God's idea." If we hope to secure that God-given freedom for the next generation of Americans, we must contend for it.

TONY PERKINS
President, Family Research Council

Dave Meyer understands that for a nation to be free, its citizens must be informed of the truth—including the truth of God's hand in history—and continually work to maintain and pass on these God-given rights and liberties. If this occurs, we can have great hope for the future. But if we neglect our duties, the fires of freedom will be extinguished.

In *Freedom Is Costly, But Priceless*, Dave clearly and succinctly presents the blueprint to follow in order to rebuild America and preserve the invaluable fruits of freedom. I believe this book will change the lives of many people and be used to help preserve the American republic.

STEPHEN MCDOWELL
President, Providence Foundation
Co-author, America's Providential History

FREEDOM IS COSTLY, BUT PRICELESS

FREEDOM IS COSTLY, BUT PRICELESS

If Not Maintained, It Will Not Remain

DAVE MEYER

WHITAKER
HOUSE

FREEDOM IS COSTLY, BUT PRICELESS
If Not Maintained, It Will Not Remain

ISBN: 978-1-64123-785-7
eBook ISBN: 978-1-64123-786-4
Printed in the United States of America
© 2021 Dave Meyer

Whitaker House
1030 Hunt Valley Circle
New Kensington, PA 15068
www.whitakerhouse.com

1 2 3 4 5 6 7 8 9 10 11 / 28 27 26 25 24 23 22 21

TABLE OF CONTENTS

FOREWORD

I have been married to Dave for 53 years, so I think it is safe to say that I know him well. I love and admire him very much. He is a man of prayer and diligent Bible study. He is disciplined, dedicated and diligent about whatever he does. I have never seen him to be more passionate about anything than he is in seeing people have knowledge of our true American history. Dave is a genuine patriot, he loves America and its people, and he wants to see the freedoms we have lost returned to us.

He knows those freedoms will not be restored, and that even more freedom will be lost, unless we learn our rights and our responsibilities concerning those rights. In this book, you will benefit from the more than 25 years that Dave has studied true American history. You will not only learn many things about our history that you may not have known, but you will know what your duties as an American are concerning the regaining and maintaining of our rights and freedoms that have been lost through a lack of knowledge and passivity concerning our responsibilities.

We are blessed to live in America, but no blessing is retained without the knowledge of how we received it and actively doing our part to keep it. We still have time to see America change for the better, but we have no time to waste in aggressively being active in learning all we can about what can be done—and then doing it.

You will be shocked concerning what has happened in our education system and the devastating effect it has had on our culture. As a matter of fact, I think you will be shocked at many of the things you will learn. Most of us complain about the government, but they work for us and we are the ones who have put our current leaders in the positions they hold. If we don't like what they are doing, complaining won't change it, but making informed decisions every time we vote will.

Dave has worked very hard on this book. I sincerely believe you will enjoy it, and that it will change your perspective about just how important each one of you are in contributing to the positive changes needed in our nation—the most important of which is to see reverence for God restored to its proper place. We only have this nation because of God, and we won't keep it without Him. As Dave states in this book, "none of us want to see what is on the other side of *too late*," so let's collectively take godly action *now* and begin to see what we have lost be restored.

Joyce Meyer

INTRODUCTION

America is a nation like no other. It was first created in the hearts of the men and women who came here from Great Britain. The colonists were guided by the providential hand of God moving upon their hearts to seek a new land where they could freely live out their faith in Him. These lovers of God looked to Him for direction, accepted His correction and expected His protection. Their faith and hope were in their God, and their love for Him was evident in their daily lives. They spoke of Him often, lived their lives by His guidance and raised their children by the direction of His Word.

Our Founders trusted God in blessed times and hard times, knowing their lives were in His hands and that all things would work out for good. They realized their lives here on earth were temporary and they looked forward to eternity. They courageously fought and gained independence when their right to freedom was challenged by their home country; then they formed a new government to protect their freedom. Their constitution was formed according to Godly principles, and therefore they prospered until they became the greatest nation the world had ever seen.

They realized that the blessed lives they were privileged to experience didn't originate from their own greatness—it was because of God's goodness as a result of their obedience to His Word.

As time passed, other people throughout the world heard of America and the blessings that God had bestowed on this great nation. As a result, many left their own countries to live in the United States. In fact, 47 *million* people immigrated to America from 1820 to 1975 in order to fulfill their dreams of living in this free and blessed country.[1]

Immigrants who came to America were required by the law to go through an immigration process. They were given a large history book that revealed how this nation was formed. And they learned how God's presence was everywhere in the birth and establishment of America because He was in the hearts of America's people. They were also given America's constitution to learn, for these would be the laws that they would be required to live by.

In 1886, a statue was erected on Bedloe's Island near Ellis Island, off the southern tip of Manhattan in upper New York Bay. It was given to America by a French sculptor named Frederic Bartholdi. He was so impressed when he visited America that it birthed a vision in his heart—to design and bless the United States with the Statue of Liberty in order to celebrate and proclaim this liberty to the world. Bartholdi spent many years traveling throughout France and sharing his vision in order to raise the necessary funds required to build the statue. Eventually, his vision became a reality. The Statue of Liberty was finally constructed, shipped to America and erected on October 28, 1886.

At the entrance of the Statue of Liberty, a sonnet is engraved on a bronze plaque. Written by Emma Lazarus in 1883, it's titled, "The New Colossus" and includes these immortal words:

"Give me your tired, your poor,
Your huddled masses yearning to breathe free,
The wretched refuse of your teeming shore.
Send these, the homeless, tempest-tost to me,
I lift my lamp beside the golden door!"[2]

It was here on Ellis Island that so many immigrants passed through immigration and were welcomed into the United States. This statement represents the heart of the American people to help others—a heart formed through the Word of God.

Jesus shares a similar statement in Matthew 11:28-30: *Come to Me, all you who labor and are heavy-laden and overburdened, and I will cause you to rest. [I will ease and relieve and refresh your souls.] Take My yoke upon you and learn of Me, for I am gentle (meek) and humble (lowly) in heart, and you will find rest (relief and ease and refreshment and recreation and blessed quiet) for your souls. For My yoke is wholesome (useful, good—not harsh, hard, sharp, or pressing, but comfortable, gracious, and pleasant), and My burden is light and easy to be borne.*

In the last 60 years, much has changed and America has been gradually slipping away from the foundation she was built upon. Her moral character is deteriorating as the Godly principles that shaped her character are disappearing. As a result, a course correction is required for America's survival.

This introduction is a brief description of America. It is our country, our home and our responsibility...and God has given each one of us the privilege to experience it and take care of it. Every generation, from the time of the colonists, has fulfilled their responsibility—*until recently.* **Now, it's our turn to preserve and pass this legacy to our posterity.**

CHAPTER 1

How Did We Get Here?

"The deterioration of every government
begins with the decay of the principles on
which it was founded."[1]
—Baron de Montesquieu,
French political thinker often quoted by the
Founders of the United States

*If My people who are called by My name will
humble themselves, and pray and seek My face,
and turn from their wicked ways, then I will hear
from heaven, and will forgive their sin and heal
their land.* —2 Chronicles 7:14 (NKJV)

This is not a political book.

And it's not even just an "American" book.

This is a *principles* book.

The United States was founded upon timeless principles, which have always been the bedrock of any

blessed society. These principles enable countries to prosper and be free, because they enable *citizens* to be free.

Regardless of your background or political affiliation, we all desire "life, liberty, and the pursuit of happiness." So, ultimately, this is a book about freedom.

Have you ever wondered about the future of your community? Do you believe our country is headed in the wrong direction, but you aren't sure how we can steer it in the right direction? Are you concerned about the society in which your children and grandchildren will live?

I am concerned. I thank God for the blessing of living in the United States, and at the same time I'm often shocked at what's happening to our country.

But I have hope—for my family, for your family and for our future.

This book is for anyone who wants to understand what's happening in the United States of America—and what we as Christians can do about it. And this is a message of hope for those in other nations who desire a brighter future.

Maybe you can trace your family tree to Europe. Perhaps your ancestors lived on this continent long before Columbus sailed to America. Your great-great-great-great-grandparents may have been brought to this continent through the evil of slavery. You or your parents may have immigrated to this country just a few years ago to seek a better life. Regardless of your background or political views, let's explore where we've been as a nation, rediscover some of the principles which unite us, and find inspiration to move forward together.

Our country is as strong as the hearts of its people. And when the people's hearts are weak, the country is weak. Hosea 4:6 clearly states, *My people are destroyed for lack of knowledge.* Ignorance is deadly to a great nation—and to each individual—because it leads to passivity, despair and hopelessness.

When you look around, do you see more and more passive, desperate and hopeless people? Sadly, I do. But it doesn't have to stay this way.

MY LACK OF KNOWLEDGE

Like most people of my generation in the United States, I was grateful for the privilege of living here, but I didn't understand much about the history of this great nation. As a result, I didn't realize the price that had been paid for the freedoms we enjoy, and I didn't know about my responsibilities as a citizen.

I knew a few stories from different parts of our history, but I didn't know the chronological history of how this country was established, the Godly wisdom that shaped our new form of government, and the amazing evidence of God's blessings.

As a young man, I joined the Army between the time of the Korean War and the Vietnam War. My decision was both productive and patriotic. During that time, in the early 1960s, if you didn't sign up, you'd almost certainly be drafted. I was given the opportunity to gain some practical career skills in the engineering field—specifically in the HVAC industry (heating, ventilation and air conditioning)—and use what I learned to help my career.

Sports were a big part of my life, so I tried out for, and made, the basketball and baseball teams. Our games were considered very important for the morale of the troops, and they certainly boosted my morale. I was stationed in France, and then Germany, and I counted myself blessed to serve the United States in those developed nations. I was also thankful to learn a lot about my chosen trade as I worked in refrigeration repair when I wasn't involved in sports.

Although I appreciated my country and served overseas, I took it for granted in many ways. That's not to say I took the men and women in our military for granted. I've always had the highest respect for those who serve our nation, and especially those who've sacrificed life and limb. If you're a veteran, active service military, a family member of someone serving, or a member of law enforcement, thank you for your service! I believe this book will be encouraging and motivating for you.

After my service—throughout my professional career and into the ministry God called Joyce and me—I had the same basic view of the United States. Then a friend sent me a gift that opened my eyes and changed my heart forever.

PROVIDENCE

In 1995, I received a small package in the mail. It was from a friend and missionary we supported who did a lot of important work in India. *What could this be?* I thought as I opened the box. In it was a book: *America's Providential History*, by Stephen McDowell and Mark Beliles.

Why would he send me this book? I wondered.

Since we were friends and sometimes played golf together, I decided to read a few pages. After all, he would probably ask me about it and I wanted to be able to tell him that I started to read it. I don't believe he knew exactly why he sent it, and I sure didn't. But God did.

Once I began to read, I couldn't put the book down. As I learned about the miraculous ways God mercifully blessed this nation, I was astounded! I'd never heard about this aspect of our history. My heart was overwhelmed as I began to realize all God had done for us, all the sacrifices our Founders made, and how the sacrifices made by so many men and women had been forgotten—or in most cases, never known.

But the effect of this new knowledge was more than intellectual; with every story I read, something stirred deep in my heart.

I wept before the Lord. Yes, I sobbed. I began to see all God had given us, and how we as a nation had forgotten what His grace had given us. I repented before the Lord and prayed, "God, forgive me for not realizing how You have blessed this nation, and forgive me for taking Your blessings for granted!"

As God opened my eyes to our past, He also helped me see where America was headed. I realized all the blessings of liberty could disappear in a heartbeat and were already in the process of vanishing.

But what could I do about it?

STEPS OF FAITH

Months went by and the stirring in my heart only grew. God was calling me to share a message.

The freedom we enjoyed as a country, if not maintained, would not remain. With all my heart I desired to move people to begin taking action. I wanted to encourage them to pray for our nation and cast an informed vote in every election. I wanted to inspire them to stand up against things that are stealing our freedom—or are morally wrong—by speaking up and contacting their senators and representatives, letting them know their thoughts on proposed legislation. People also need to stop voting for candidates who make promises that they don't fulfill. We need people in political offices who honor God's Word, and we need to hold politicians accountable to do what they promised.

The price of peace is eternal vigilance. The loss of peace is a result of eternal negligence. All who enjoy the right to live in freedom must also be willing to fight for freedom. Freedom is never free; the price is constant stewardship.

I'll admit that I was nervous about sharing this message. In my mind, I felt unqualified and probably a bit like Moses when he was called to speak and said, *"O my Lord, I am not eloquent"* (Exodus 4:10 NKJV). I was not a teacher like Joyce. I had this passion in my heart but it felt difficult to express. And there was opposition, as there always is in a battle.

Would people understand that my message wasn't about a political party, but about patriotism?

Maybe you've had the same questions as a believer— and the same reluctance to speak up for freedom and Christian values. I understand completely. But let me also share that this hesitation is part of the reason we've seen our country decline in so many ways. While we wonder about what to do, how to do it, or if we should do *anything*, our culture moves further from its original foundation. And the effect is a loss of freedom and opportunity for every American.

Many Christians have been wary of addressing issues with our government because they view it as politicizing the Church. But I wasn't getting "political," I was trying to help people understand our civic responsibilities as Christians and recognize what a gift it is to do so.

If we don't fulfill our Christian civic responsibilities, we will lose our rights as recognized by law. And if we lose our rights, we lose the ability to speak freely and legally share our faith. And I'm sure you've noticed, this is the direction our country has been drifting for quite a while.

Even today when I share with Christians how many of our public schools are not teaching the truth about our founding, and are even telling students that our nation is evil, the typical response is, "Really? I had no idea."

I'm not judging educators or citizens. In fact, I had a similar view before I learned the truth about our history. And I assumed this country would keep growing and fulfilling its vision of life, liberty and the pursuit of happiness.

Since the very beginning of our nation, parents wanted their children to read. They knew if their children could read the Bible, they would have a strong foundation for life. When we as a nation started to establish public schools, the teachers were often Christian ministers. Most of our leading universities—including

Harvard, Yale and Princeton—were founded by ordained ministers. Through the 19th century, most of our universities had Christian roots and Christian presidents.

Those facts surprise most people today. What happened over the past several decades to change our nation in such drastic ways? We, as a society and as Christians, assumed everything would be okay.

That's why our country's Founders constantly taught vigilance and civic responsibility. They knew something I didn't understand fully, until I gained knowledge of our *true* history.

Our second president, John Adams, said, "Our Constitution was made only for a moral and religious People. It is wholly inadequate to the government of any other."[2]

HOW DID THIS COUNTRY GET HERE?

One day I was praying for our country and said, "God, You are the answer to all our nation's problems."

In my heart, I heard loud and clear, "No, I'm not! You are. The American people are the answer to their problems. If they will learn and fulfill their responsibilities, their problems will disappear."

As I pondered further, I understood that if "we the people" in this blessed country will learn and fulfill our responsibilities, most of society's problems would disappear. God will be *with us* in our responsibility, but He will not fulfill our responsibility *for us.*

Second Chronicles 7:14 says, *If My people, who are called by My name, shall humble themselves, pray, seek, crave, and require of necessity My face and turn from their wicked ways, then will I hear from heaven, forgive their sin, and heal their land.*

God is basically saying, if we will do what we can do, He will do what only He can do. As outlined in this Scripture, our part follows these lines:

Realize something's wrong and humble ourselves.

Humble ourselves and let humility first drive us to prayer.

To seek God's face means to ask, "What's my problem, God? What do I need to do, or stop doing?"

Turn (repent)—taking action to move away from what's wrong and toward what is right.

Many believers read the verse this way: "If My people pray, then I will heal their land." They fail to see the dual responsibility of their part *and* God's part, and the importance of the word "then." The word "then" reveals that God's part does not start until our part has been completed. Our part is to humble ourselves (realize something is wrong), pray and seek (for God to reveal what the root issue is) and turn (repent and go in the right direction). Then, and only then, will God fulfill His part to hear, forgive and heal.

Too often Christians pray, but they fail to fulfill their responsibilities and then wonder why their prayers were not answered.

We often pray about what we want *God* to do, but we sometimes are not seeking what God wants *us* to do. We have a moral crisis in our nation and each one of us is responsible to live our lives in a way that glorifies God and upholds His principles. If all Christians do this, we will see a quick turnaround in our nation.

What can we do about our community and our country? It starts with gaining knowledge and truth. Without information there can be no motivation, and without motivation there can be no activation. And unless we put this knowledge into action, our nation will not heal.

THE CYCLE OF FREEDOM'S DESTRUCTION

How our great nation is in the process of being destroyed! But it does not have to stay this way if we will heed the warning...if we will learn and fulfill our responsibilities through the correct knowledge of our history. Knowing our true history is the only way we can know our identity as Christian citizens of this great nation that God has given us the privilege to live in. It's the only way of knowing our responsibilities so we can protect our rights.

Let's start with why our history is so important.

Our history identifies God as the source of our nation's greatness. But without this knowledge, many have been deceived through our educational system into believing that *we* are the source of our greatness. This is called humanism (man replacing God), which is the beginning of what I call the "cycle of freedom's destruction" in any Christian nation.

In a Christian nation, wherever there is a lack of knowledge concerning its heritage, there will also be an abundance of deception masquerading as truth. Deception is a lie disguised as truth by the arrogant— or truth disguised as a lie—and accepted as truth by the ignorant. Since our history has been revised, our wisdom has been deleted and our direction has become disoriented.

As I have studied our beautiful yet seldom-known American history, the following is what I believe God has revealed to me as "the cycle of freedom's destruction." I could have called it "America's progression into regression."

Each downward step in this cycle could be a book.

Since our history has been revised and made our nation unwise, truth has been disguised. It's hardly recognized; therefore, many people are paralyzed as our morals are criticized, because our wisdom that was once highly prized is now despised, and we the people have been compartmentalized (categorized). Consequently, good is desensitized, and as a result, right is compromised and wrong is not penalized. When right is compromised and wrong is not penalized, our rights are jeopardized because many of our laws have been neutralized (no longer enforced); therefore, without resistance, evil is energized. Since our laws have been neutralized, evil is eventually legalized, then freedom is marginalized, patriotism is ostracized (banished), and hope dies as tyranny (unlawful rule) is realized and bondage arrives.

Each of these categories is prevalent in our nation right now and moving forward rapidly.

When history is unknown, a desensitized person or nation instinctively and intuitively sees something is wrong but lacks the knowledge—and therefore the wisdom—of what to do. As a result, they do nothing. Consequently, this wrong, which was once highly detested, eventually becomes part of everyday life. Wrong has been transformed into right through compromise because of ignorance.

Therefore, wrong is not penalized. And when right is compromised and wrong is not penalized, the standard of right deteriorates, and its power and authority are diminished until eventually wrong replaces the standard of right.

When wrong replaces the standard of right, evil is energized and eventually legalized, since all resistance to evil was removed when good was desensitized; right was compromised, and wrong was no longer penalized. Therefore, our rights were jeopardized because our laws were neutralized.

We have reached a time in history where we are becoming hopelessly and helplessly lost, and the sad and scary part is that we have become accustomed to it. We are living in denial of our condition, because we see no solution; therefore, we accept survival in place of revival. The price of survival is the compromise of our principles. It requires no effort on our part, but its cost is our freedom.

The price of revival is costly. It requires our effort to learn our history, which will cause us to repent for our lack of knowledge and learn how to become responsible, which in turn creates revival and produces restoration.

Our civil government was ordained and established as our servant to protect our rights and maintain law and order so we, the people, might enjoy a peaceful life. For our civil government to remain our servant, we, the people, were entrusted with the responsibility of its maintenance. To fulfill this obligation, we as individuals were required to know how our government worked and what our responsibilities were.

This responsibility was fulfilled by the people of America for a century and a half, as each generation was taught the importance of maintaining what God had given them through their Founders (by their knowledge of their true Godly history).

Then, in the 1930s and continuing to this day—even though there are many good educators—our public education system was hijacked by Marxists, humanists and socialists. They revised our history, removing God from our history books, and programmed most of society into ignorance. Their goal is for us to be passive as our rights are removed without opposition. Through the controlled educational system, they have trained much of the media to twist the truth and deceive the general public. This creates a clear path for carrying out their socialist agenda.

Romans 13:3 reveals the importance of our civil authorities: *For civil authorities are not a terror to [people of] good conduct, but to [those of] bad behavior.*

Since evil has been legalized and our laws have been neutralized, the respect for our civil authorities has deteriorated and justice is being compromised. Unlawful behavior is more prominent today than it was 50 years ago, because unlawful behavior is not penalized today like it was then. The reason is that non-enforcement of the law creates lack of respect for the law and deterioration of society's behavior.

Why would a great nation like America allow its history to be revised? It was done without our knowledge. While we as a nation were asleep (passively ignorant), our children in each generation were being programmed into ignorance through our humanistically controlled educational system. This has been going on for so long that almost everyone 50 years of age and younger does not know our true history. How better to control a people than as Karl Marx, author of *The Communist Manifesto*, reportedly stated:

"Take away the heritage of a nation and they are easily persuaded."[3]

I would add that they will believe whatever they are told, and will be easily deceived and easily persuaded to forfeit their rights without resistance. They will believe anything and stand for nothing.

In writings from the 1700s, *The Decline and Fall of the Athenian Republic*, Sir Alexander Fraser Tytler, a history professor at the University of Edinborough, is known to have listed the "Cycle of Nations." The average age of the world's greatest civilizations is 200 years, and they have all passed through the following sequence.

If you know anything about America's history, you will recognize the progression and regression of our nation in this sequence. You may also recognize what stage America presently occupies. Here is the sequence:

From bondage to spiritual faith.
From spiritual faith to great courage.
From great courage to liberty.
From liberty to abundance.

(Now watch the transition.)

From abundance to selfishness.
From selfishness to complacency.
From complacency to apathy.
From apathy to dependency.
From dependency back to bondage.[4]

Our nation is one step from bondage as our dependency is shifting from God to government without knowledge of how this is happening. The question is how and why we regressed into this condition.

The answer is found in what happened between abundance and selfishness. We began to take the blessings of God for granted and were no longer thankful—and when we are not thankful we stop being responsible. The lack of remembrance of how our nation progressed from bondage to abundance can only be found in our true and accurate history. Without a thankful heart and a responsible attitude, neither America—nor any nation—has the ability to remain great. And without knowledge of their history, no nation has the ability to be thankful and responsible.

This is how America is in the process of being destroyed. But we don't have to stay that way if we will educate ourselves.

In a parable recorded in Matthew 13, Jesus describes a man who has a good field, bearing good fruit. He awakened one morning to find his field filled with tares, weeds and bad fruit. How did his field change from good to bad? In Matthew 13, Jesus identifies the problems. While good men slept, the enemy planted the tares. Jesus never faulted the enemy for what they did. The problem was good men went to sleep. They were not active when they should have been.

Inactivity to protect what is rightfully ours equates to loss of liberty, and loss of liberty equates to bondage.

It was this danger of good citizens going to sleep that most concerned our early American leaders and should concern us today. They understood that if we were inactive, our government would become corrupt and tyrannical, resulting in political slavery of its citizens. Only if its citizens remained alert and active stewards could this condition be avoided.

When the history of a nation is unknown, citizens

can no longer be alert stewards. They no longer know how to protect their rights and maintain their authority.

Ignorance of freedom's responsibilities guarantees eradication of freedom's rights.

Without accurate education (which reveals knowledge, promotes dedication, creates responsibility and protects rights) there can be no preservation, and therefore continuation, of freedom.

If we will learn and fulfill our responsibility, we will have the eligibility of casting our care, as John Hancock stated after signing the Declaration of Independence. I call this statement the reward of a patriotic citizen:

> "And having secured the approbation [approval] of our hearts by a faithful and unwearied discharge of our duty to our country, let us joyfully leave our concerns in the hands of Him who raiseth up and pulleth down the empires and kingdoms of the world as He pleases."[5]

FREEDOM AROUND THE GLOBE

I vividly remember the first time Joyce and I went to India to minister in 1980. It was like being on a different planet. India is unlike any place on the face of the earth. Living conditions range from primitive to modern. The sights and sounds of the cities are intense.

As someone who appreciates cars, I thought the traffic was, and is, unbelievable. There are rickshaws, cars, trucks, motorcycles and bikes on the street—along with cows and even elephants. And it seems like everyone in motorized vehicles honks their horn every 30 seconds. By the way, I've asked friends from India who moved to the United States if it was difficult to not use their car horn while driving here. Everyone said yes!

Every society has differences and similarities. In India, as in each of the over 100 countries where we share the Gospel, the people are wonderful. But, sadly, it's also evident that most people have never experienced life with a government established on principles of individual freedom. The poverty is crushing, and the look of hopelessness on people's faces is too common.

We've hosted conferences in India with hundreds of thousands of precious people in attendance. Most walk miles and miles to hear the Word of God. They are hungry for freedom—spiritually and in their everyday lives. And thanks to God's grace and our faithful ministry partners, we're blessed to carry out our work in India to this day, boldly proclaiming the message of freedom. We hope millions and millions of people in India, and every country on earth, will discover their freedom in Jesus Christ and let their light shine in their communities—including in their local and national government.

We also work in countries with Christian roots, many in Europe. And, sadly, we've seen how these societies have drifted away from their history and Godly principles. In many cases their Christian heritage is being replaced by secularism, humanism and socialism, which results in a loss of freedom.

They're hungry for true freedom. But they've rejected, and not remembered, the source of freedom. It's a preview of where America is headed.

But it doesn't have to be this way. Freedom is available to every person and every society. But freedom is costly.

Twenty-five years ago, a book changed my life. At first, I was a bit fearful about sharing this message.

That was then. This is now.

I'm not nervous. In fact, I'm more emboldened now than ever.

What made the difference? Knowledge.

CHAPTER 2

What We Have Is
What We've Allowed

"The only thing necessary for the triumph
of evil, is for good men to do nothing."[1]
—Edmund Burke

*Blessed is the man who walks not
in the counsel of the ungodly....*
—Psalm 1:1-2 (NKJV)

It's not always easy for us to recognize our nation's drastic moral decline, but wherever we look, reverence for God has been removed from our government and nearly every aspect of society.

I celebrate the many advances our country has made, but what breaks my heart is the devastating effect that secularism has on people's lives. We want every human being to enjoy the life Jesus died—and rose again—to give us. Allowing more and more legal and cultural restrictions on our expression of faith has not helped people live abundant, peaceful lives. I'd argue the effect is quite the opposite.

Yes, there always has been opposition to freedom and to Godly principles, and there always will be. But to a large extent, these negative changes happened—and shifted at an alarming rate—because we allowed them. We should have opposed them vehemently, letting our politicians know that we did not want changes that would remove God from society and steal our religious liberties.

Before we examine our current situation, let's look back a few centuries.

In the early decades of our country, many professing Christians tolerated policies and practices that violated biblical principles. Some of the injustices included slavery, segregation, treatment of Native Americans, and non-equal rights for women.

This certainly does not apply to all Americans, or all Christians, during these periods of our history. There were many believers who stood up to injustice, and we're thankful they did. Many brave Americans risked their livelihoods and sacrificed their lives for the cause of "liberty and justice for all." Over two million Union soldiers were mobilized during the Civil War, and almost a half million Union soldiers gave their lives. Most, if not all, of those who dedicated their lives to abolishing slavery were Christians. And Christian abolitionists were active on this continent since before the United States declared independence.

The Declaration of Independence is the document describing the founding spirit of our nation. It clearly speaks the truth when it says that "all men are created equal, that they are endowed by their Creator with certain unalienable Rights, that among these are Life, Liberty and the pursuit of Happiness."[2] However, these injustices took too long to be addressed and corrected.

The Bible clearly shows God's heart when it comes to these matters of equal treatment: *There is [now no distinction] neither Jew nor Greek, there is neither slave nor free, there is not male and female; for you are all one in Christ Jesus* (Galatians 3:28).

There was no excuse for not standing up to the wrongs in our society then. And there's no excuse now.

In the early 1930s, four major shifts happened almost simultaneously in our country.

THE GREAT DEPRESSION

The stock market crashed in 1929 and in the blink of an eye, a quarter of the working population was without a job. In the months that followed, panic ensued, followed by desperation. This caused American minds to be open to massive changes in government and society.

THE GREAT DECEPTION

People cried out—not to God, but to the government. In 1933, in response to the economic collapse, President Franklin D. Roosevelt introduced the New Deal, a plan for the federal government to meet the needs of the people. This began the decline of the "old" deal (God's deal) where reliance on God was the norm and the Church provided for many of the needy.

Instead of being skeptical of this "solution" and viewing options through the lens of Godly wisdom, Americans embraced the giveaways, which have only increased year after year to this day.

I believe the president thought he was helping our struggling nation. However, when the New Deal was enacted, the Church in many instances became passive in their previous habit of helping the poor and needy. God designed us, the Church, to show forth our love and fulfill this responsibility.

After the New Deal was enacted, the traditional responsibility of meeting the needs of the people shifted from the Church to the government. This was the beginning of "big government."

THE GREAT POSSESSION

Marxist, humanist and secularist radicals began to infiltrate our public educational system in the early 1930s.

Christians were largely unaware, and as a result, did not stand against it. Academically, America was once ranked at the top of nearly every category worldwide. However, since this concession of our educational system, our numbers have fallen across the board, and we are now 38th in math and 24th in science.[3]

The intentional efforts to undermine America's moral and spiritual roots started in 1933. In order to escape Hitler, a group of Marxist German intellectuals came to America at the invitation of John Dewey, who was on staff at Columbia University and a self-described "democratic socialist."[4]

Dewey is known as "the father of modern education." However, most people don't know he was the father of "progressive" education, which emphasized humanism. He was also a signatory on the *Humanist Manifesto 1*, published in 1933, and with the help of his friends throughout American universities, he strategically placed thousands of like-minded men in teaching positions—specifically in education and journalism. He knew the most effective way to instill his worldview into millions of Americans was through the classroom and the media.

What did they teach? Dewey's method was to place greater value on physical and emotional experiences over facts and practical knowledge. Dewey's method rejects history, tradition, and cultural and moral values in favor of "diversity" and "tolerance." Little by little, his appointed group of teaching pioneers chipped away at the moral fiber established by our Founding Fathers.

The results were devastating to our nation. By the 1960s, the seeds of his philosophy grew into a counter-cultural revolution, resulting in anti-God and anti-American sentiment. Young people openly rejected the morals of our past and embraced the feel-good experiences of the present, opening the door for increased drug use and immorality.

Many of those young people became the university presidents, professors and authors of our children's textbooks. And we wonder why our history has been distorted and rewritten!

We have been just like the proverbial frog in the pot of water: Instead of realizing what was happening and jumping into action, it was slowly and passively boiled to death. The temperature increased gradually, and it never realized what was happening.

THE GREAT CONCESSION

Cole Porter's 1934 hit song "Anything Goes" actually celebrated the moral collapse of America as moral relativism was taught to our youth. One line even states, "Nobody will oppose." Generally speaking, he was right.

In just four years, the landscape of the United States shifted.

"Give me four years to teach the children and the seed I have sown will never be uprooted."[5] This statement was made around the same time by Vladimir Lenin, the Russian communist revolutionary who established what would become the Soviet Union.

SEPARATION AND MISEDUCATION

Another major cultural development occurred in 1947. Most people have never heard the name Hugo Black. However, Supreme Court Justice Black decided the First Amendment of the Constitution needed to include a wall of separation between the church and the state. The truth is, our Constitution does *not* mention "separation of church and state" or even imply it—nor do any of our founding documents.

None of the court's precedents, which were only briefly mentioned, required this result. The case was an official betrayal of America's Christian heritage. The judicial branch of our government cannot make laws. Only Congress—the legislative body—can. However, Justice Black, who served in the judicial branch of our government, made that decision. And we allowed it to become the law of the land because of a lack of opposition. A nation that does not stand for its rights is forced to live without them.

The First Amendment states, "Congress shall make no law respecting an establishment of religion, or prohibiting the free exercise thereof; or abridging the freedom of speech, or of the press; or the right of the people peaceably to assemble, and to petition the Government for a redress of grievances."[6]

In common-sense language, our Constitution tells Congress to stay out of religion and the free expression of faith in God. With the wide acceptance of the myth of "separation of church and state"—and the misinterpretation of the crucial First Amendment of the Constitution—the Church took another step back from society and civic involvement.

Why were those who wanted to change this country so intent on "separating" the Church from civic life? Because the Church is the conscience of our country. When Justice Black shut out the Church, the enemy shut down our nation's conscience.

Evil gains ground where there is no opposition.

STUDENTS DIDN'T HAVE A PRAYER

Sacred ground was again lost in 1962 when the courts ruled to remove prayer from schools. Tragically, the Church stood by silently and watched it happen. Sure, there were a few who made some noise, but no unified, sustained action was taken to prevent this loss. Brainwashed by the lie of "separation" and an increasingly secular culture, most parents did not stand against the change.

As reverence for God and His Word was removed from the classrooms of our nation, the SAT scores plummeted and have never recovered. At the same time, moral decline, violent behavior, and the breakdown of the family increased dramatically. And these trends continue.

I'm certain that allowing godlessness to expand into our communities, schools and government is not what Jesus meant when He spoke about turning the other cheek.

We, as individuals and as a nation, have been intentionally programmed into ignorance in order to be induced into sleep (passivity) so we might be indoctrinated into bondage.

When we are uninformed, we are desensitized. When we are desensitized, we are disengaged. When we are disengaged, we passively watch our rights disappear without resistance.

The following quote is often attributed to Benjamin Franklin: "A nation of well-informed men who have been taught to know and prize the rights which God has given them cannot be enslaved. It is in the region of ignorance that tyranny begins."[7] This means a nation of uninformed men who *don't* know and therefore can't prize or protect the rights that God has given them can and will be enslaved.

In the 1950s and '60s, the cultural-demise envelope was pushed even further when our government (under pressure from special interest groups) began to remove all references pertaining to God—and stories of our Godly heritage—from our history books.

I'll never forget how I felt when watching a talk show host several years ago. He was upset about a tragic current event in our country and asked, "Where was God in all of this?" Almost without thinking, I exclaimed, "Right where we put Him"—which was out of our history, schools and government.

Yes, we have pushed God out of our history, out of our schools and out of our government. Then, when situations go wrong, people blame God for not protecting us. We forget: When any nation expels God, they also expel His protection.

God alone is the reason the United States has been the most blessed nation on earth. However, we can't continually push Him away and expect to continue to enjoy His blessings. We can still turn things around and regain what we have lost, but it will require that every citizen do their part. Each vote is important, each prayer is important, and every time anyone speaks out to maintain our religious freedoms, they are fulfilling their God-given, and therefore God-required, responsibilities.

PARENTS AND PREACHERS

The two main ways we can regain, and then maintain, our freedom in this country is through the crucial role of parents and preachers. As I look back over my life as a father and teacher of my children, I see where I could have done a better job in educating and motivating them. And maybe we could all agree, generally speaking, that pastors, teachers and parents have not addressed the changes happening in society and government as effectively as we could have.

I'm certainly not judging or placing condemnation on anyone. As I detailed in the previous chapter, I was simply ignorant about our country's history. My role as a Christian is to be engaged in our government, because it was designed to be operated "by the people and for the people."

The reason more parents and preachers have not talked much about the remarkable history of this country is simple: They, like me, did not know our history. If we don't know our founding principles, we can't fully recognize the dangerous changes in society and know what to do about them. Again, this book is not about politics; it's about knowing where we came from and what God intended for this country so we can stand for what is right and oppose what is wrong.

When I first started writing and speaking about this subject, I would often say, "We've forgotten our history." But that's not true. In most cases, people have not forgotten our history—they have *never known* our true history.

PROMISES VERSUS PRINCIPLE

Here's a pop quiz for you. Is the United States a democracy?

Of course, our country is widely believed to be a democracy. But there's one big problem with that belief: Our government is not a democracy and never was. We are a constitutional republic.

Democracy is rule by a majority. A republic is rule of law.

Our Founders understood the difference, and they hated the concept of democracy. They had lived under the tyranny of a monarch but were equally wary of the tyranny of the *mob*. In a true democracy, the majority rules. In a republic, the law rules—and elected leaders are entrusted to execute or change the established laws.

Why is "majority rule" potentially bad? Imagine if a majority of people believe socialism is good and private property—and private enterprise—is bad. Regardless of the laws in place to protect property owners and their heirs, the majority mentality would overrule the law.

Benjamin Franklin is often quoted as saying, "When the people find that they can vote themselves money [from the treasury] that will herald the end of the republic."[8] If you pay attention to any political debate, you'll see his warning applies to our political system today. People will vote for promises over principles because they believe they will get something for free. But the government can't give anyone anything unless it first takes from someone else.

The Founders didn't envision a government that would provide money or other benefits to its people. Their dream was a place where people could enjoy something much better: *Freedom.* They longed for a place where people could dream and then accomplish amazing things through hard work. All people want equal *rights*, but they don't all want equal *responsibility*, and that was not God's intention for this great nation.

OUR DECLARATION

Those who want to dismantle and destroy our country's foundation seem to ignore the amazing words in our founding document, the Declaration of Independence.

"We hold these truths to be self-evident, that all men are created equal, that they are endowed by their Creator with certain unalienable Rights, that among these are Life, Liberty and the pursuit of Happiness."[9]

When I see angry people who hate our country, I think, *They must have never read those words—words that declared a belief in God's goodness and the value of every human being.*

There is no other government on earth that was founded on these principles of freedom. It's no wonder the United States has grown and prospered for so long, provided an unparalleled standard of living for hundreds of millions of people, and helped make the world a better and freer place.

But the sad fact is, in many ways, we've allowed the country to drift from the powerful principles it was founded upon. We have allowed the separation of church from state, instead of enthusiastically engaging in Christian civic responsibility. These responsibilities include voting for principled candidates, holding our elected officials accountable to maintaining our Constitution, and standing against anything that steals our rights.

More and more churches have stopped speaking about our founding principles of freedom. They have stopped encouraging people to resist policies which are wrong and will eventually steal our freedom. And a growing number of parents have not known how to teach these truths to their children.

The Revolutionary War was fought for freedom. Our Declaration of Independence cites 27 grievances why the colonials demanded independence. The signers and citizens put their lives on the line, fought the greatest fighting force on the face of the earth at that time, and won. This victory was a miracle, made up of countless other miracles, as our nation was formed.

After our Constitution was written, it's reported that a woman asked Ben Franklin, "Well, sir, what have you given us?"

He answered, "A republic, if you can keep it."[10]

Franklin understood what too few understand today. Independence does not endure without each individual's personal responsibility.

THE CONSENT OF THE GOVERNED

The Declaration of Independence goes on to state that governments derive "their just powers from the consent of the governed."[11] Think about that bold statement for a moment.

Instead of a king imposing power on people, this new government derived power from the consent—agreement and authority—of its citizens. What an amazing gift. And what a profound responsibility.

A main cause of the current problems in America is that the *governed*—you and me and our neighbors—have often failed in our responsibility to fulfill our civic duty. Instead, many of us have been passive. Because anytime there is ignorance (a lack of knowledge) concerning our history, our rights and our responsibilities, it often leads to passivity in those areas.

We have a government of the people, by the people, and for the people; therefore, the politicians work for us. If we don't like how our elected representatives are doing their job, it's our job to replace them.

There are three requirements for a Christian nation to be destroyed:

1. Christians become passive.
2. Voters become ignorant.
3. Leaders become corrupt.

It all starts with passive Christianity. When active Christianity deteriorates, resistance to voter deception disintegrates and opens the door and invites corruption in to leadership. When and where evil is exposed but not penalized, it becomes energized and eventually legalized. When evil is exposed but not punished, freedom forfeits its right to exist!

In a constitutional republic, all people must come under the jurisdiction of the law. When violators of the law are not prosecuted, the Constitution will be dismantled by those in authority who fail to carry out their responsibilities. Consequently, they will forfeit their authority, allowing the destruction of the Constitution through passive compromise.

In a constitutional republic, good does not compromise with evil and remain in control. Over the years, responsible active evil has grown in America as irresponsible inactive good has withdrawn.

The Bible teaches that during the New Millennium (the Millennial Reign of Christ on the earth), Jesus will reign with a rod of iron (see Revelation 2:27). I interpret this to represent enforced authority and power.

Peaceful authority can only be maintained by the display and enforcement of power.

I've heard the statement "peace through power," and I believed it. I now know this is a wrong statement. A true statement is, "peace through *enforced* power." Peace is not possible when power is not enforced. Evil only flees when confronted by force.

Freedom is a result of the price that was paid by the men and women who paid that price at the time it was required. And it only remains when that price *continues* to be paid. If we turn our backs on freedom's responsibility, freedom will turn its back on our protection.

When a person or nation does *what* it should do *when* it should do it, it's much easier and much more effective than trying to do what it should have done and didn't do until years later. Why? Because God's grace coincides with God's timing. God's grace, if applied when required, prevents Satan from getting a foothold that can become a stronghold in the future.

In America today, passive "consent" and a wrong view of "tolerance" have weakened our fulfillment of the responsibility of the people; therefore, we are relinquishing much of the freedom we once possessed and enjoyed.

Have you ever noticed that those who demand tolerance never seem to *tolerate* expression of Christian faith in society? Instead, they want to use tolerance to celebrate immoral behavior and expect us to agree with them. We cannot separate God from our government. America was built on principles of faith in God's Word and cannot be maintained if those principles are ignored.

FOUNDING PRINCIPLES

There's a battle for the principles on which this nation is founded, because God's principles and God are inseparable. The Bible teaches us Godly principles. His principles are His guidelines that provide direction for people to make right choices. What happens to people and nations that follow God's guidelines and make right choices? Both the Bible and history reveal the results.

They prosper, deal wisely and have good success.

This Book of the Law shall not depart out of your mouth, but you shall meditate on it day and night, that you may observe and do according to all that is written in it. For then you shall make your way prosperous, and then you shall deal wisely and have good success (Joshua 1:8).

MEDITATE, OBSERVE AND DO

How do you destroy an exceptional nation? You attack

its foundation. You start by redefining our Founders' moral character and mocking the Godly principles that citizens have lived by. You emphasize its wrongs and leave out its rights; in other words, you share the part of the truth that fits your agenda.

Once these lies, perpetrated to destroy the character of our Founders, have been imbedded in the souls of our young people (our children), they are taught to disrespect—and possibly even hate—their country because they believe it was built by bad people with evil motives.

Because the United States was built upon God's principles, it was known to be exceptional—not only by Americans but throughout the world. In fact, it was so exceptional that from 1820 to 1975, 47 million immigrants left their country to live in and become citizens of the United States. But now in the eyes of many people—including many of our young people—America has become evil and unexceptional. This is because their knowledge of the past and God's hand in American history has been distorted as our history has been revised. Things that are negative in our past have been magnified, while the overwhelming abundance of our positive history has been erased.

This is the way to keep Godly principles—the principles that our exceptional nation was built upon—from the lives of our children. It's the way to destroy patriotism and replace it with socialism.

You're probably familiar with the term "outsourc-ing" in reference to businesses sending jobs to other companies or other countries. In the past hundred years, we've outsourced vital areas of our society:

We've outsourced education from parents to the government.

We've outsourced morality to popular opinion.

We've outsourced care for the poor from the Church to the government.

BLESSED

As Christians, we are called to let our lights shine and love our neighbors. This includes loving and praying for those who are ignorant of—or acting as enemies of—the truth. My heart goes out to those who are deceived and think wrong is right, and those who seek to under-mine this country's foundation. They're missing out on God's blessings.

We must love them in word and action. But this doesn't mean we must allow their agenda to go unchallenged.

Our motivation is love. We can show love, while disagreeing and being active in preserving biblical truth.

We can oppose abortion—and not tolerate govern-ment funding of it—but love and support mothers who might be considering it. We can choose to not accept certain practices or curriculum in our schools, but we can love our teachers and those who are responsible for the curriculum.

Psalm 1:1 declares, *Blessed (happy, fortunate, prosperous, and enviable) is the man who walks and lives not in the counsel of the ungodly [following their advice, their plans and purposes], nor stands [submissive and inactive] in the path where sinners walk, nor sits down [to relax and rest] where the scornful [and the mockers] gather.*

The scornful counsel of the ungodly is taught in too many of our classrooms, reported as truth on television, and streamed into our mobile devices. We must decide to stop "following their advice, their plans and purposes" and stop allowing ourselves to be "submissive and inactive." It is very dangerous to passively believe everything you read without seeking the knowledge of whether or not it is actually true.

God is waiting to help us fulfill our responsibility. He wants us to be *blessed*. But this particular blessing awaits those who "walk and live" according to Godly principles. Instead of passively *allowing* wrong behavior to continue unchallenged, let's start taking our responsibility and *doing* what needs to be done to see our nation return to its moral foundation.

★★★

CHAPTER 3

Why Liberty and Freedom Are Vital

"Our lives begin to end the day
we become silent about things
that matter."
—Dr. Martin Luther King, Jr.[1]

It is for freedom that Christ has set us free.
—Galatians 5:1 (NIV)

Freedom. Liberty. Two of the most stirring words I know. And they've come to represent many of the good things this nation stands for. Millions have fought for freedom. And every Memorial Day, we honor the millions who have *died* to protect our freedom.

Contrary to popular belief, liberty was not "made in America"—it is a gift from Almighty God.

This goes all the way back to the Garden of Eden. When God made Adam and Eve, He made them in His image. He gave them liberty—and the ability to govern themselves and everything else God created.

You see, liberty always moves from the *internal* to the *external*. It must first begin in the hearts of individuals, and then it will express itself externally in all aspects of society. A society is a reflection of the condition of the hearts of its people.

Are freedom and liberty the same? Commentary in *The Founders' Bible* makes this distinction:

> Don't they largely mean the same thing? They are indeed synonyms: and yes, given their interchangeability in language, in many respects they often refer to the same general concept. But in the minds of many of our Founders, there was an important distinction. Freedom is defined as "independence, the licenses to do as one wants, the permission to do as you please."[2] It means you have the right to do something, a clear measure of granted authority or autonomy for self-determination or self-government: but it has one potential deficiency—it can also be narrowly defined as only having permission to do it. Permission is necessarily granted by someone, which means freedom can be revoked by that someone.
>
> While to some it may seem like an unnecessary splitting of hairs, liberty, while meaning much the same thing, carries with it one particular irrevocable

nuance of profound implication—it has everything to do with the source.

Thomas Jefferson described liberty in the Declaration of Independence when he wrote that "all men are endowed by their Creator with certain inalienable rights." Liberty, second only to life, is a right endowed by the Creator. It is a part of you, just as are your mind, will, emotions and spirit. It cannot be legally revoked. Liberty provides for the protection of an individual's rights, expressly because with it we have been endowed by our Creator with the capacity for self-government. Freedom is something that a government grants; liberty is something we own that a government cannot take away.[3]

We can forfeit liberty, but no one has a right to take it away from us.

Second Corinthians 3:17 says, ...*where the Spirit of the Lord is, there is liberty* (NKJV). When the Holy Spirit comes into the heart of a person, that person is liberated. Likewise, when the Spirit of the Lord comes into the fabric of a nation, *that nation* is liberated. There is a direct relationship. The degree to which reverence for God is infused into society—through its people, laws and institutions—is the degree that citizens will experience freedom in every realm: civil, justice, religious and economic.

In his famous "I Have a Dream" speech in 1963, Dr. Martin Luther King, Jr. references the Declaration of Independence and the United States Constitution in regard to our heart's cry for freedom:

> "When the architects of our republic wrote the magnificent words of the Constitution and the Declaration of Independence, they were signing a promissory note to which every American was to fall heir. This note was a promise that all men would be guaranteed the inalienable rights of Life, Liberty, and the pursuit of Happiness."

He began the address by saying, "I am happy to join with you today in what will go down in history as the greatest demonstration for freedom in the history of our nation."

Dr. King closed with these words: "And when this happens, when we allow freedom to ring, when we let it ring from every village and every hamlet, from every state and every city, we will be able to speed up that day when all of God's children, black men and white men, Jews and Gentiles, Protestants and Catholics, will be able to join hands and sing in the words of the old Negro spiritual: 'Free at last! Free at last! Thank God Almighty, we are free at last!'"[4]

Our Constitution is one of the most highly regarded documents in history, yet our Founders knew this document alone couldn't save us. They knew the future success of America would hinge entirely on adhering to the biblical principles it was founded upon—then teaching these principles of freedom to the next generation. After all, their desire for freedom is what fueled the revolution to begin with. In truth, the revolution began long before any of the fighting ever started.

We have a responsibility to understand freedom from a Christian perspective and take every opportunity to cultivate the God-given desire for freedom in the hearts of people.

WHERE DO FREEDOM AND LIBERTY COME FROM?

Freedom is not an American idea. It's God's idea.

Freedom is the ability to do as one pleases, within helpful boundaries. As God told Adam and Eve, "Enjoy this all-you-can-eat buffet. It's free! Just stay away from this one tree" (Genesis 2:16, paraphrase). This boundary was for the good of God's children. And in a free society, laws are important for the good of its citizens.

Today, we in America often take our freedom for granted. We enjoy the ability to live as we please within the confines of the law. Our laws actually protect us and protect our freedoms.

In Romans 13:3, the apostle Paul writes, *For rulers are not a terror to good works, but to evil. Do you want to be unafraid of the authority? Do what is good, and you will have praise from the same* (NKJV).

I know, it's somewhat ironic that to enjoy freedom, there must be laws. However, we need boundaries because of the fallen nature of humankind. And we need people to enforce our laws—for our protection.

Since evil has been legalized and many of our laws have been neutralized, respect for our civil authorities has deteriorated and justice is being compromised. This is why unlawful behavior is more prominent today than it was 50 years ago. Non-enforcement of the law creates a lack of respect for the law and for those who choose to protect and serve us—the men and women of law enforcement.

When a society becomes *more* lawless, its people enjoy *less* freedom.

The law is designed to protect, not oppress, freedom.

THE PRICE OF FREEDOM

There is always a price for freedom. In the case of our nation and our fellow citizens, a high price was paid for our freedom. In the United States, our basic laws and freedoms were written into the Constitution and based on the principles in the Declaration of Independence.

When the Founders saw that some basic rights were not addressed in sufficient detail, they amended the Constitution. For example, the First Amendment reads:

"Congress shall make no law respecting an establishment of religion, or prohibiting the free exercise thereof; or abridging the freedom of speech, or of the press; or the right of the people peaceably to assemble, and to petition the Government for a redress of grievances."[5]

The Founders wanted to make sure Congress would not interfere with free expression of faith and speech—and the freedom to *peaceably* assemble. They didn't set up an official government religion, as many monarchies had done. Nor did they want limits of religious expression, as many monarchies had imposed on their people—the way many governments do today. They knew that the free practice of Christianity would help the country thrive.

Today, we see the rise of humanism and secularism. In my view these are a form of religion, because they are based on the *belief* that there is no God. More and more, the government seems to be "respecting an establishment" of these religions and disrespecting Christianity.

What are we to do about this trend? The first step is to recognize it.

RIGHTS AND FREEDOMS

According to our founding documents, we have the right to practice our faith, speak our views freely, and peacefully assemble, along with many other rights.

But if we do not continually protect our rights, we will lose them.

As in the court case that led to the false claim of "separation of church and state," we see that if we're not vigilant, those who want to silence Christian expression and influence will gain ground.

From a global standpoint, and in our experience as a ministry working in many countries, we see how the lack of a Christian foundation in government policy and culture adversely affects people. Countries that don't allow Christian principles to shape their laws and policies always slip into more and more government control—with fewer and fewer rights for citizens. We've seen this in third-world nations and in some parts of Europe.

Let me be very clear that I'm not being judgmental about the people in these countries; it's the principles— or *lack* of biblical principles—that are to blame. When this happens, people suffer unnecessarily.

For example, we once traveled to Papua, New Guinea, and held a huge conference. The people there loved Joyce's teaching. While we were there, we learned that it was not uncommon for husbands, even Christian husbands, to beat their wives. As you might imagine, Joyce addressed that situation directly and boldly—and with the authority of God's Word. She told the men that the custom was directly against God's principles and contrary to God's beautiful vision for marriage.

We heard many great reports from that conference—from both men and women whose lives were changed for the better based on understanding God's principles. Cultures change, but God's Word remains the same forever. When a nation's laws and policies are based on a biblical foundation, people's lives are simply better. When a nation's laws and policies shift from that foundation, they must be addressed for the good of every citizen.

WHY FREEDOMS COME AND GO

I recently read an article published by the American Family Association. The article cites research on the rise and fall of civilizations, conducted by two secular scientists in the early 1900s. Here's an excerpt:

> One of the scientists was J.D. Unwin, a British anthropologist who wrote *Sex and Culture* (1934). The other was Pitirim Sorokin, founder of the sociology department at Harvard University, who wrote *The American Sex Revolution* (1956).
> They independently studied the process by which

these cultures/civilizations decayed and died—or survived. They asked this question: can decaying cultures rebound? Their answer: yes—it's rare, but possible.

Here's what they said: in societies that recovered, there was a small segment of the people that remembered the process by which the society had grown strong and prospered. To rebuild it, those people must be willing to:

• Stay faithful to these ideas and steward them—teaching the next generation;
• Avoid the temptation to join the party, participating in the decadence; and
• Endure the ridicule, persecution and even violence from the broader society that rejects the "old ways."

When reality crashes in, they said, the revelers will look for answers—and often turn to this small group of cultural "outcasts." Even though Unwin and Sorokin were secularists, their descriptions of the only ways a decaying culture could reverse course sounds amazingly similar to the words of Jesus in Matthew 5:13-16, where our Lord calls us to remain salt and light.

In other words, many people will finally realize that culture has deteriorated into insanity. Those who have "not conformed to the world" will stand out as a beacon of hope (see Romans 12:2; Matthew 5:13-16). This is a huge lesson for believers in this country.

I saw this same truth in effect when I worked at an engineering office. I stood up under cultural conditions that were often against my beliefs and against the principles I valued. There were about 65 other men in my department, and before I left the company I had the opportunity to work directly with every one of them. I believe the hand of God was moving me around so I could be a light to them.

First, my new coworkers would test me. For example, one man started to tell me a dirty joke and I interrupted him, saying, "You know what I believe in and what I stand for. Why would you try to tell me something like that?"

I would never change the way I treated them, with respect and kindness. But I was clear about what was acceptable for me.

Then, when some of their lives were falling apart because of problems in their marriage or other personal crises, they came to me and asked for prayer. I had the opportunity to share my faith and the message of Christ with many people during that time and it was a blessing. When we stand up for our Christian principles, people may make fun of us or even join in persecuting us, but they also respect us.

Yes, it was sometimes difficult, and I had to stand strong—and walk in love—for a long period of time. But the effort was worth it, because it helped other people and brought glory to God. I also believe that my stand changed the culture of that workplace and directly affected my and Joyce's destiny, by the grace of God.

Freedom comes—and remains—based on our courage to stand up for Godly principles.

In a sermon preached in 1814, Reverend Jesse Appleton said, "It is the immutable purpose of God, that a people, destitute of moral principle, shall be neither free nor happy."[6]

Whatever is ordained must be maintained if it is to be sustained and ultimately retained.

CASE LAW OR CONSTITUTIONAL LAW?

The legitimacy of any law is revealed in its enforcement. When a constitutionally based law is misinterpreted by the courts, its original intent is diluted and therefore not enforced. If a law is not enforced, its validity is destroyed and the freedoms it protects become more vulnerable.

When a court ruling departs from interpreting the law—according to the original intent of the

Constitution—and begins to, in effect, *make* laws, this is known as "legislating from the bench." When a judge wrongly interprets a law and that wrong interpretation is unchallenged by the legislative branch of our government, in practical terms it replaces the true law. This new law, now considered "case law," is taught in place of *constitutional law* in most of the law schools in our nation.

In many of America's law schools and courtrooms, "case law" has replaced "constitutional law." Consequently, the original intent of our Constitution has been marginalized. In other words, when legal cases are decided without honoring the clear language of the Constitution, justice is not served.

According to our Constitution, only the legislative branch has the authority to make laws.

So, when case law replaces constitutional law, the judicial branch of our government has usurped the authority of the legislative branch.

With little or no knowledge of what is being taught in the law schools of our nation, society has accepted the deception that case law replaces constitutional law. The root cause is that we have elected leaders who allow, and in some cases celebrate, this departure from our founding documents.

We are a government of the people, by the people and for the people. That means our elected leaders work for us. It's time for us to learn and fulfill our Christian civic responsibilities and re-establish the authority of our Constitution.

The United States was formed as a constitutional republic in the historical context of a Christian society. The pyramid of authority in this form of government is, from top to bottom: God and His Word above all, then the law (beginning and ending with the Constitution), followed by the government (we, the people), and finally the elected leaders (who are employed by the people to govern according to the original intent of the Constitution).

A law, regulation or guideline is only as strong as the enforcement of it. Without its enforcement, its power and authority disappear.

For example, freedom of speech and freedom of assembly are cornerstones of our nation.

FREE SPEECH AND FREEDOM OF ASSEMBLY AT THE UNIVERSITY OF VIRGINIA

In a recent case, the Leadership Institute (Leadership-Institute.org) stood up for our free speech and free assembly rights at the University of Virginia. Here's their story:

> From the beginning of The Burke Society's existence, a conservative student organization at the

University of Virginia (UVA), the group faced various barriers because of their principles. From tactics the students learned from Leadership Institute, membership has gone from 15 students in 2008 to 40 members, plus an email list of over 300.

When The Burke Society applied to become a recognized student organization by the UVA student government, they were denied on the basis of discrimination because the students wanted to study conservative thought. The founders of The Burke Society promptly contacted Leadership Institute for advice and support. The Leadership Institute referred the students to a legal organization, which sent a letter to UVA's president on behalf of the students, threatening to sue because UVA is a public university where students have constitutional rights to free speech and association.

The university president quickly informed the liberal student government they had to approve The Burke Society as an officially recognized organization.

When the group wanted to publish a conservative student publication, Leadership Institute was there again with training and a grant to help offset the cost of their first issue. The Burke Society students found out UVA offers students a class devoted to modern liberalism. Subsequently, they wanted the school to balance the political spectrum and establish a class devoted to conservatism.

After their first request for a class in modern American conservatism was rejected without reason by the student government, The Burke Society again requested help. Leadership Institute held a campus election workshop at UVA to train students how to win student government elections, and unseat those who rejected their application. During the training, Leadership Institute staff worked with students to develop additional strategies and approaches to get the course approved.

Finally, after a year-long battle with the administration, The Burke Society was able to secure a class on Modern Conservatism at UVA which began 2010. The students incorporated readings they were studying in their meetings and worked with professors to draft an in-depth syllabus.

Registration for the modern American conservatism class quickly surpassed the 30 student maximum capacity, and the university gave The Burke Society permission to increase the size of the class.

Their ultimate goal was to expand this course to other schools around the country. Working with Leadership Institute, the class has been taught on a number of campuses since 2010 and has grown to offer online courses.[7]

FREEDOM MUST BE PROTECTED

Our Constitution is marginalized when our elected leaders in Congress relinquish their rightful authority to make laws—and when we do not hold them accountable.

Our government is being hijacked because more and more of "we the people" are ignorant of the fact that *we* are the government and are the stewards of the legal freedoms established in the Constitution.

We must stop blaming "the government" if we are not willing to fulfill our responsibility.

The following quote is often attributed to Benjamin Franklin: "A nation of well-informed men who have been taught to know and prize the rights which God has given them cannot be enslaved. It's in the region of ignorance that tyranny begins."[8]

As Americans, we must become educated or we will be subjugated, and our freedom will be eradicated.

Bondage is always preceded by complacency, and complacency is always preceded by ignorance. If we don't remember who we are, we won't know how to stand up for our freedom. A complacent Church and a Christian nation cannot coexist. The Body of Christ has two choices—either learn and fulfill our responsibilities or relinquish our freedom. We cannot remain silent and remain free.

The future of America is in the hands of those who

act or those who watch. What America will look like tomorrow, next month or next year will be decided by those who engage—or by those who stand on the sidelines as spectators. If you love your country and value your freedom, the one place you don't want to be is on the sidelines, and the person you don't want to be is a spectator. The problem is most people are on the sidelines wandering aimlessly without a clue that their freedom is disappearing. It is time for the Body of Christ to become the Army of God and fulfill its Christian civic responsibilities.

A world without God and His Word is a world without freedom. The freedom God desires every person and every nation to experience is dependent upon each individual's and nation's ability to function according to His principles.

CHAPTER 4

A Fresh Look at History

"A nation which does not remember
what it was yesterday,
does not know what it is today,
nor what it is trying to do."[1]
—Woodrow Wilson,
the 28th President of the United States

I remember the days of old;
I meditate on all Your doings;
I ponder the work of Your hands.
—Psalm 143:5

As a young child, I wasn't interested in history. Maybe your experience in school was similar to mine. Most of what I learned about history seemed to be random facts and dates—an incomplete timeline or random stories of our country. As a result of this scattered information,

I didn't comprehend the amazing way our nation had developed—and I didn't fully appreciate it.

Understanding the sequence of events is what made our history come alive to me as a clear and complete picture developed and revealed God's guiding and protecting hand on our nation.

America's history, when delivered truthfully and accurately, is not boring. Nor is it just a class you take in school. History gives direction for now and is our platform of guidance into our future. How we choose to utilize the rich history of this country has implications on today and tomorrow. Remembrance is essential in our society for the people to be free and prosperous. One can't remember what they've never learned. And no one can stand up for what they don't know.

HISTORY REVISED AND ERASED

"I have but one lamp by which my feet are guided,
and that is the lamp of experience.
I know no way of judging the future but by the past."[2]
— Patrick Henry

Throughout the last several decades, the Godly heritage of our nation has gradually and systematically disappeared from our classrooms. Reverence for God has been removed from our schools and our American history has been revised. What was once a beautiful, exciting story is now unrecognizable.

How can what we used to teach as history, only half a century ago, suddenly disappear? *How* and *why* has so much of the truth been replaced with information that is actually false?

It's inspiring to see how God's words and our beliefs are literally inscribed on government buildings and monuments throughout our nation's capital. Yet, at the same time, the mere mention of God has been removed from public school history books and from many history books available in secular bookstores.

There is an agenda in this country to erase God and Christian principles from our way of life—even if it means taking bold, unconstitutional measures to change our laws. It's something our Founders warned us about.

Since true and accurate history is a nation's platform for the future, the nation's path to the future will become dysfunctional without accurate information. I call this *historical amnesia.*

History is a flow of events that begins with the creation of time. It reveals the providential hand of God as events are acted out on the stage of life. And history is the story of the good and bad choices of people. If recorded accurately and truthfully, it is the story of who we are and the *when, where, why* and *how* events took place. History not only teaches us what to do, but also what *not* to do. I can look back at my own personal history and easily see the result of right decisions, but I can also see the result of wrong decisions. I learn from history what destroys and what brings success and enjoyment.

If history is not recorded in the order it happens, it is not history but simply a listing of random events without continuity. When this occurs, the providential hand of God is no longer identifiable and our understanding of historical events becomes chaotic and confusing. Without truthful, accurate history, the direction for the future becomes unclear because pieces of the past are missing. People and nations lose their way and destinies are unfulfilled.

When the truth of history has been discarded, deleted or revised, nations are destined to go through the same tragic and costly situations over and over again. History repeats itself, nations are destroyed because of ignorance, and people suffer needlessly.

The Bible teaches in Proverbs 3:13: *Happy (blessed, fortunate, enviable) is the man who finds skillful and godly Wisdom, and the man who gets understanding [drawing it forth from God's Word and life's experiences].*

Today, our children, grandchildren and even great-grandchildren are often taught an incomplete or incorrect view of our nation's history. When our schools were overtaken by humanism, secularism and socialism, our education system and our history were slowly revised. In some cases, important elements were erased completely from classrooms.

First, the Christian faith of our nation's Founders was undermined by merely and wrongfully referring to them as "deists." (A deist refers to someone who might believe in a "higher power" but does *not* acknowledge Jesus Christ as Lord and the Bible as the inspired Word of God.) Eventually, their positive contributions to a growing republic were undermined by those who painted them with a broad brush and labeled them inhumane racists. All of our Founders were not perfect, and like any human they made mistakes. But they sacrificed greatly in order to give us a government that would provide opportunities for us to succeed in life, as long as we are willing to follow Godly principles and work diligently in our chosen field. It is dangerous to focus on the mistakes of some and, in the process, throw out the good choices of the majority.

Remember, those who try to take reverence for God out of public life need to first dismantle the foundation—our principles and those who wrote them into law.

When I was in school, American history wasn't

necessarily taught in a patriotic way, but there was emphasis on the truth and the unique, positive aspects of our country. In other words, students were taught that the United States is an exceptional country—especially when compared to other nations in history—because of God's influence. I was never taught that America was perfect, but I knew we had a government founded on timeless principles. And when those ideals were implemented and honored, those principles would continue to bring about liberty and justice for *all*.

As time progressed, those with an anti-American worldview gained more control in our public education system and the media. And the changes in how history was taught happened so gradually that most people didn't even realize what was taking place. Most parents didn't know what was happening, and far too many still don't realize how far institutions and standards have changed.

Along the way, something else happened. History itself was disrespected.

Why does this matter? An accurate understanding of history makes the difference between life or death and good and evil—for a country and its citizens.

There is an attack on history, because an understanding of history can help people see God's hand on the earth: creation, the rise and fall of leaders, the blessing and destruction of societies, the wisdom of honoring God, the foolishness of rejecting Him and, most of all, the grace of God that is offered to us through Jesus Christ.

THE HISTORY OF HISTORY

I want to share with you an important definition from Webster's 1828 Dictionary. However, first, let's take a quick look at what *America's Providential History* says about Noah Webster himself.

Webster worked about 26 years on his *An American Dictionary of the English Language*. By the time of its completion and publication in 1828, Webster had mastered 28 languages. This colossal work reflects the diligence, scholarship and Christian character of this great yet humble man.

His dictionary, which was the first American dictionary and the grandfather of all others, defines words biblically and generously uses scriptural references. The present-day dictionary that bears Webster's name is a good example of how education has been secularized. A comparison reveals that not only have thousands of Scriptures been removed in modern editions, but biblical definitions have been replaced by definitions reflecting humanistic thought.

Noah Webster's life can be characterized as prolific. In addition to his dictionary and textbooks—the

Blue-Backed Speller, *Grammar* and *Reader*—he wrote on a number of topics including religion, politics, education, music, economics, commerce, medicine, society and science. He was also the first person to publicly promote the idea of a constitutional convention.

His efforts brought about copyright legislation at state and national levels. He served in state government, published a magazine and newspaper, founded a college, and translated the first American revised version of the Bible. While doing all these things, his family was not neglected as he lovingly raised seven children!

It was men like Noah Webster who educated the generations of Americans that secured this country as the most free and prosperous nation the world has seen.

Now, in light of what we know about Webster's character and accomplishments, let's look at the definition of *truth* in Webster's 1828 Dictionary: Truth is "Conformity to fact or reality; exact accordance with that which is, or has been, or shall be. The truth of history constitutes its whole value, honesty; virtue, real fact; real state of things."[3]

The truth of history reveals right as right and wrong as wrong. The deception of history, which eliminates truth, reveals right as wrong and wrong as right. Therefore, history without truth becomes a weapon to destroy good and encourage evil. Consequently, the truth of socialism, which throughout history is revealed as evil, is now taught and accepted as good in our public educational system.

This is how a conservative constitutional republic (freedom) is transformed into a radical socialistic tyranny (unlawful rule) with little or no opposition. Society becomes a prisoner of its own ignorance.

The concept of history, and the importance of knowing our true and accurate history, was ingrained in the culture of our country from its very foundation. This is why the Bible was often used in education.

The Bible is emphatic on the importance of knowing and understanding history. For example, the book of Job, 8:8-15, reads:

For inquire, I pray you, of the former age and apply yourself to that which their fathers have searched out, for we are but of yesterday and know nothing, because our days upon earth are a shadow.

Shall not [the forefathers] teach you and tell you and utter words out of their hearts (the deepest part of their nature)? Can the rush or papyrus grow up without marsh? Can the flag or reed grass grow without water? While it is yet green, in flower, and not cut down, it withers before any other herb [when without water].

So are the ways of all who forget God;' and the hope of the godless shall perish. For his confidence breaks, and [the object of] his trust is a spider's web. He shall

*lean upon his house, but it shall not stand; he shall hold
fast to it, but it shall not last.*

Did you catch the meaning of those metaphors?

We are told to "apply" ourselves to that which our
fathers (and mothers) have searched out. Because without that knowledge, we "know nothing."

We need people to teach and tell us true history,
because it's our foundation for right living. Plants can't
grow without soil and water, and we can't flourish
without the knowledge and wisdom that comes from
knowing our accurate history. Without this knowledge,
we have no confidence in anything we build or lean on.

In addition, reading Deuteronomy Chapter 32
provides a passionate sermon on the importance of
history.

AMERICA'S ROADMAP TO FREEDOM

It was September 17, 1787. The Constitutional Convention was wrapping up in Philadelphia, and the delegates
each took their turn signing a document that would
forever change the nation—*The Constitution of the
United States of America.*

Benjamin Franklin sat and took it all in, then once
again found himself staring just past the president's
chair at a familiar painting of a warm sun gleaming
above the horizon.

"I have often in the course of the Session looked without being able to tell whether it was rising or setting," said Franklin. "But now at length I have the happiness to know that *it is a rising sun.*"[4]

Everyone understood his meaning—he believed the Unites States would succeed. In fact, the document Franklin and his friends gave us that day was a roadmap to freedom, resulting in the greatest nation in history: a rising sun poised to shine brightly.

That day in 1787, we officially became a republic—a nation based on law, and many of those laws were based on Scripture. Our government locked many Godly principles into our Constitution. The results were astounding. From before our founding to today, many of our leaders and citizens honored the Lord as the only source of good, and we quickly became a nation of abundance.

Most of our government buildings have Scripture inscribed in their walls. In addition, all courtrooms once had the words "In God We Trust" presented on the wall behind where the judge sat—that is, until one particular judge ruled that the public should no longer have to endure the sight of those distracting and misleading words while in court. I think his ruling is one of the most pathetic statements I have ever read. Being able to trust in God is a privilege, not something we have to try to endure!

The Ten Commandments were once prominently displayed in our schools and various other public places. But these displays are disappearing as ungodly and immoral people fight to have them removed. It is time for those who believe in and love God to take a stand for these time-honored displays so they can remain where they are for all to see.

Facts of interest:
- 47 million immigrants came into our country from 1820-1975.
- Equality of rights for women and other groups were legally protected.
- The United States represents approximately 5% of the world's population but has created more new wealth than the rest of the world combined.
- We are responsible for more discoveries in medicine, education, power-energy, transportation, aircraft and agriculture than any other nation.
- The United States has been the food basket of the world, and we have never suffered a famine.
- We are always the first to provide relief to other nations during natural calamities, sometimes even providing aid to our enemies.[5]

Many consider a republic to be the highest form of government devised by man. However, it also requires the greatest amount of human care and maintenance. If neglected, a republic can deteriorate into a variety of "lesser" forms...

- A democracy—a government conducted by popular feeling
- Anarchy—a system in which each person determines their own rules and standards
- Oligarchy—a government run by a small council or a group of elite individuals
- Dictatorship—a government run by a single individual

Our republic was formed for good, moral, *active* people. However, over the years, our moral fabric has deteriorated and the American people have lost their way and slowly stopped fighting for what's right.

Our passivity has come at a great price. In the past 60 years alone, we have allowed God to be erased from our history books, prayer to be taken from our schools, and the government to exercise unprecedented control over our everyday lives.

America has experienced unparalleled *abundance*. But as we began to forget the Source of our abundance, selfishness and greed have reared their ugly heads. We have gone from being a strong, Godly nation—ready to fight for our liberties and moral principles—to one that's *complacent,* allowing ungodliness to creep in little by little.

Today, we are a nation that doesn't even know there is a battle raging because we're ignorant of our history. As a result, we are yielding our rights and slowly becoming more dependent on the government—not God—as our source.

Ignorance is what has caused America to lose its way; however, *accurate knowledge* is the key to finding our way back.

WE NEED WISDOM

When the history of a nation is removed from the people, the removal of their rights and authority will soon follow. This will be done slowly, silently, secretly and systematically, so the people do not become alarmed and rise up against it.

A nation without its history is destined for doom.

When history is known and understood, the people have the ability to maintain their freedoms and, consequently, protect their rights. Wherever there is a lack of knowledge, there is an abundance of deception masquerading as truth.

There is a treasure hidden in the history of every nation. This treasure has a name and reveals the devastating condition of a nation when God's Word was known but not applied. This treasure also reveals the extraordinary effect on a nation when the Word is known and its principles are *applied*. A nation is blessed when its people properly apply these Godly principles and cursed when they do not apply them. Only if the application is changed will the future of that nation change.

Throughout history we see nations moving from blessed to cursed, or cursed to blessed, as they move between the application and non-application of God's Word. Over thousands of years of history, what we do *not* see is the continued application of God's Word. If we did, that nation would continue to exist and would continually be blessed—and be a blessing to the people. America still has the opportunity to be that nation, but only if she learns her history.

What is the treasure in every nation's history? This treasure is wisdom.

When a person understands the chronological time-line of a nation, including the pivotal choices of leaders and citizens, wisdom is revealed. (There are blessings when God's Word is applied or curses when it is not.)

History is our teacher; it reveals consequences of good or bad choices. It can give or withhold direction, correction and protection depending on our knowledge or ignorance of it. When history is ignored, forgotten or revised—and therefore never known—we lose our direction, don't know what is correct, and are open to deception, therefore forfeiting our protection as a result of our wisdom being discarded.

THE ENEMY OF WISDOM

Deception is wrong perception due to bad conception of truth. It's the enemy of wisdom.

Deception is a lie conceived, disguised, delivered and achieved as truth by the arrogant, because it is perceived and received as truth by the *ignorant*.

Deception cannot exist in an atmosphere of true knowledge. It can only exist in an atmosphere of ignorance. In an atmosphere of knowledge, deception is exposed and evicted. Therefore, the spirit of deception constantly searches for an atmosphere of ignorance.

The end goal of deception in a Christian nation is removal of God and loss of rights and freedoms.

Each right represents a portion of our freedom. For example, we have the right to freely worship, speak and congregate, along with the right to a fair trial in a court of law, to name just a few. When God-given rights are not maintained in our country, that portion of our freedom disappears.

Whose responsibility is it to maintain our rights? *We the people* of the United States of America.

But we can't maintain our rights if we don't know them or if we are ignorant of the Godly principles on which they are based. Do you value your freedom?

The proof is in how you take care of it.

History is our textbook, our compass, our guide.

History defines our rights and reveals our responsibilities.

History is a treasure of wisdom.

History reveals consequences of good and bad choices, which provide valuable wisdom.

For the most part, the Body of Christ knows little or nothing about its amazing, extraordinary American Godly heritage. Consequently, they are untrained, unequipped and unqualified to function as the Army of God and fulfill their Christian civic responsibilities. As a result, they are unknowingly forfeiting their rights and authority—and therefore their freedom.

America's condition, that once was very clear, is now confusing. God's story was once our story. But since the truth of our story is missing, our history that once gave clarity to our destiny has now become a mystery.

The statement below is the answer God revealed to my heart in capsule form as I was meditating on America's present condition.

"Lose our history, lose our way, live in misery.
Find our history, find our way, live courageously.
Find our way, find our destiny. Find our destiny,
and we've solved the mystery.
The truth of history reveals that God's desire for our

destiny is now and has always been for His-story to be our story for His glory."

If our history is reinstated as His-story, our courage will be revived to fulfill His desired destiny for our lives.

We must know the past to understand the present and secure the future. No recollection of the past means no direction for the future; and no direction for the future guarantees a dysfunctional destiny. But most people have been taught false history in which God has been removed. Therefore, they have no desire to hear about history, because when we take God out of it, we remove the life in it and history becomes dull and boring.

When you add God back into the story of our nation, history once again becomes His-story. History is no longer boring, but educational and inspiring.

WHERE DO WE BEGIN?

You already have access to the most amazing history book: the Bible. Yes, the Bible is the inspired Word of God, but it's also a riveting account of the history of mankind.

Do you want to understand how and why nations rise and fall? Study the Bible.

Are you hungry for wisdom on the subject of leadership? Study the Bible.

Are you wondering how Christians can influence governments and cultures for good? Yes, study the Bible.

It's easy to see why the Bible was the first book to be removed from public education. Without it, our view of American history is shallow and incomplete.

And it's obvious why there's an attack on teaching true and accurate history. If we don't understand our past, we will be susceptible to deception about our present—and make foolish choices about our future.

Most Americans don't have the slightest idea of who we once were as a nation. All they know is they don't like who we have become and feel hopeless and helpless to change it.

When it comes to knowledge of our rich Godly heritage, most Christians are poverty-stricken and therefore too paralyzed to respond to issues that are stealing our God-given rights. We have an identity crisis because of historical amnesia, and therefore we are living a dysfunctional lifestyle as our national debt *increases* because our national morals have *decreased*.

History defines our rights and reveals our responsibilities. Knowledge of our rights and action concerning our responsibilities determine the quality of our freedom. When history is unknown, our rights are redefined and our irresponsibility is revealed. The quality of our freedom deteriorates and the America we once knew begins to fade and gradually disappear.

Proverbs 11:11 says, *By the blessing of the influence of the upright and God's favor [because of them] the city is exalted, but it is overthrown by the mouth of the wicked.*

Notice this verse does *not* say, "by the blessing of the upright the city is exalted." It reveals that the city is exalted due to God's favor because the upright were influential. It also reveals that the city is overthrown when the upright are lacking in influence. This means there is no resistance to evil when Christians are not influential; they leave a void that will be filled with evil activism.

FAITH IN ACTION

Ronald Reagan made this profound statement in his California gubernatorial inaugural address on January 5, 1967:

"Perhaps you and I have lived with this miracle too long to be properly appreciative. Freedom is a fragile thing and is never more than one generation away from extinction. It is not ours by inheritance; it must be fought for and defended constantly by each generation, for it comes only once to a people. Those who have known freedom and then lost it have never known it again."[6]

What America will look like next month, next year and beyond will be decided by those who engage or those who passively stand on the sidelines. Our freedom requires a tithe of our time to learn our true history and fulfill our responsibilities. The future of America as a free and blessed nation is dependent upon the time we as citizens of this great nation are willing to invest in learning its history. Our decision directly affects our future fate.

Before you can *be* responsible, you must learn *how* to be responsible.

When the people have knowledge,
the eyes of vision are clear.
The heart of hope beats true.
The muscles of faith are strong.
The spirit of love willingly and courageously pays whatever price is required for the life of freedom to be maintained.

If the Body of Christ is not activated, its voice will be terminated. Our voice is our choice to use or lose. God's Word and an accurate account of our history reveal that if we will do our part, God will do His part.

History is His-story.

History has our backs if we don't turn our backs on His-story.

The future is always an extension of our past. If our past is distorted and God's handiwork has been removed, our direction for the future will disappear and we will wander aimlessly—just as the Israelites did each time they forgot God. The result is always the loss of freedom.

On the other hand, if we will remember our past and all the great and mighty acts God has done, we will no longer be deceived. We will gain wisdom and begin to actively take back what has been stolen.

CHAPTER 5

The Word of God as Sacred History

"Those who cannot remember the past are
condemned to repeat it."[1]
—George Santayana

In addition to being the inspired Word of God, the Bible is an amazing history book. We can view the Bible as a rich historical record, full of wisdom about the rise and fall of countries, leaders, governments and societies.

The centerpiece of His-story is Israel. In the book of Deuteronomy, God commanded Israel to *remember* the mighty miracles He had done for them—and instructed the Israelites to teach them to their children:

And when Moses had finished speaking all these words to all Israel, he said to them, Set your [minds and] hearts on all the words which I command you this day, that you may command them to your children, that they may be watchful to do all the words of this law.

*For it is not an empty and worthless trifle for you;
it is your [very] life. By it you shall live long in the
land which you are going over the Jordan to possess*
(Deuteronomy 32:45-47).

Have you ever tried to teach a person about a subject
you didn't know or understand? The lesson doesn't go
well, does it?

That's why it's so important to know and understand
the Bible. And when it comes to the subject of government and citizenship, we would be wise to glean the
lessons from both the Old and New Testaments. They
contain God's principles on how to live a blessed life.

TWO EQUALLY IMPORTANT HISTORY BOOKS

Many Christians read and study the New Testament
but don't invest time in the Old Testament. The Old
Testament is vitally important because it shows God's
loving engagement with His people and a *nation*.

When you read the books of Kings and Chronicles,
a simple pattern emerges from generation to generation: When leaders obeyed God's principles, the nation
was blessed. When they did not, the nation was cursed.

The New Testament has also influenced and transformed societies and governments. Jesus famously
said, "*...give back to Caesar what is Caesar's, and to
God what is God's*" (Matthew 22:21 NIV). He did not

tell His followers to ignore governments and their legal authority. We are supposed to serve God and respect government, and we can do both.

The apostle Paul and the early Church interacted with their government on a frequent basis, and their witness completely transformed the Roman Empire. Paul was a Roman citizen and was taken to prison and beaten. When he informed his captors about his rights as a citizen, they became afraid, because punishing a Roman citizen in this way was illegal. Paul leveraged the law and government authority to protect his rights, and his case was eventually appealed all the way to Rome.

It's an undisputed historical fact that the government of Rome went from persecuting Christians to eventually adopting and promoting Christianity throughout the Roman Empire.

The United States' legal system was based on and influenced by the Word of God. The principles in the Word of God were central to the Declaration of Independence and the Constitution. If there is no standard for order, there will be a standard for disorder. Sadly, we see that today in many of our large cities.

Witnesses in court cases were asked to place their hand on a Bible and promise to "tell the truth, the whole truth, and nothing but the truth, so help me God."

One could also argue that representative government began when Moses' father-in-law suggested, *"Moreover you shall select from all the people able men, such as fear God, men of truth, hating covetousness; and place such over them to be rulers of thousands, rulers of hundreds, rulers of fifties, and rulers of tens. And let them judge the people at all times. Then it will be that every great matter they shall bring to you, but every small matter they themselves shall judge"* (Exodus 18:21-22 NKJV).

Each leader represented a certain number of people and was responsible under God and under Moses to make right decisions. And the Bible contains clear warnings about what happens when we are ignorant of God's principles and don't live by them. The Bible shows that God foretells history!

THE HISTORY OF THE FUTURE

In Deuteronomy Chapter 30 (NKJV), God clearly outlines what will happen if His people choose His way, and what will happen if they don't. Take a moment to carefully read the chapter below. As it says, the commandments are "not too mysterious" to be understood. In fact, they are crystal clear.

"Now it shall come to pass, when all these things come upon you, the blessing and the curse which I have

set before you, and you call them to mind among all
the nations where the Lord your God drives you, and
you return to the Lord your God and obey His voice,
according to all that I command you today, you and
your children, with all your heart and with all your
soul, that the Lord your God will bring you back from
captivity, and have compassion on you, and gather you
again from all the nations where the Lord your God
has scattered you.

"If any of you are driven out to the farthest parts
under heaven, from there the Lord your God will gather
you, and from there He will bring you. Then the Lord
your God will bring you to the land which your fathers
possessed, and you shall possess it. He will prosper you
and multiply you more than your fathers. And the Lord
your God will circumcise your heart and the heart of
your descendants, to love the Lord your God with all
your heart and with all your soul, that you may live.

"Also the Lord your God will put all these curses on
your enemies and on those who hate you, who perse-
cuted you. And you will again obey the voice of the
Lord and do all His commandments which I command
you today.

"The Lord your God will make you abound in all
the work of your hand, in the fruit of your body, in the
increase of your livestock, and in the produce of your
land for good. For the Lord will again rejoice over you

for good as He rejoiced over your fathers, if you obey the voice of the Lord your God, to keep His commandments and His statutes which are written in this Book of the Law, and if you turn to the Lord your God with all your heart and with all your soul.

"For this commandment which I command you today is not too mysterious for you, nor is it far off. It is not in heaven, that you should say, 'Who will ascend into heaven for us and bring it to us, that we may hear it and do it?' Nor is it beyond the sea, that you should say, 'Who will go over the sea for us and bring it to us, that we may hear it and do it?' But the word is very near you, in your mouth and in your heart, that you may do it.

"See, I have set before you today life and good, death and evil, in that I command you today to love the Lord your God, to walk in His ways, and to keep His commandments, His statutes, and His judgments, that you may live and multiply; and the Lord your God will bless you in the land which you go to possess. But if your heart turns away so that you do not hear, and are drawn away, and worship other gods and serve them, I announce to you today that you shall surely perish; you shall not prolong your days in the land which you cross over the Jordan to go in and possess.

"I call heaven and earth as witnesses today against you, that I have set before you life and death, blessing and cursing; therefore choose life, that both you and

your descendants may live; that you may love the Lord
your God, that you may obey His voice, and that you
may cling to Him, for He is your life and the length of
your days; and that you may dwell in the land which
the Lord swore to your fathers, to Abraham, Isaac, and
Jacob, to give them."

God gave believers a multiple-choice exam, and
then gave them the answer: Choose life!

The history of the Bible shows that any time Israel
followed the principles that God taught them, they
were blessed. The same blessings also applied to other
people and nations who honored God, His Word and
Israel. The Bible is a history book that tells us how
to be blessed—as a society, personally and in our
families.

Because family structures have broken down in
recent decades, many of the blessings that were previ-
ously passed down from generation to generation
have been cut off. The parents no longer know and
understand how to live a victorious, blessed life, so
they are unable to pass the principles on to their children and grandchildren. Today it is not uncommon
for parents to choose to work more hours in order
to have more things, as opposed to spending time
with their children and teaching them biblical principles they should live by. Families spend less time

together and more time on social media and television programs. Even families eating meals together is rare these days, but just a few short years ago the evening meal was one of the main family events of each day.

PREDICTABLE RESULTS

Multiple times in the book of Deuteronomy, Israel was commanded to love the Lord and obey His written commands. They were commanded to impress all that God had done for them upon the minds and hearts of their children. They were warned to not forget God and His law when they entered the Promised Land.

A short time later, as recorded in Judges Chapter 2, we see how long this lasted.

> *So the people served the Lord all the days of Joshua, and all the days of the elders who outlived Joshua, who had seen all the great works of the Lord which He had done for Israel. ... When all that generation had been gathered to their fathers, another generation arose after them who did not know the Lord nor the work which He had done for Israel (Judges 2:7,10 NKJV).*

As amazing as it might seem, in spite of God's warning, it only took one generation for Israel to forget God and forget how He had blessed them. If this decline happened to Israel, how much more vigilant must we be?

The moral decline we see in this country, and many other nations, is mainly due to the fact that fewer and fewer people know their history and understand the Bible's wisdom as it pertains to society, laws and leadership.

OUR MORAL STANDARD DETERMINES OUR GOLD STANDARD

Moral failure occurs when moral people fail to maintain the moral standard—usually due to silence because of ignorance, which results in irresponsibility.

Moral failure results from the loss of principles in the fabric of the lives of the people, and therefore the culture, of a nation. Moral character has a higher value to a nation than intelligence. When its moral character is no longer identifiable, the social structure of the nation disappears.

Whenever and wherever national morals in any nation have decreased, the national debt will increase, because without morals there are no restrictions to confine corruption.

America's national debt problem is a result of the decay of America's national morals. If we will restore our national morals, the national corruption and resulting national debt will disappear.

THE UNITED STATES AND THE BIBLE

"We cannot read the history of our rise and
development as a nation, without reckoning with
the place the Bible has occupied in shaping
the advances of the Republic."[2]
— President Franklin Roosevelt

Rather than the anti-Bible sentiment we see from our
government in recent decades, the first leaders of the
United States recognized the unique value of the Bible.
My friend David Barton relates this story about how
Congress and other Founders took measures to make
sure our citizens had access to the Word of God.

Prior to the American Revolution, the only English
Bibles in the colonies were imported either from Europe
or England. Publication of the Bible was regulated by
the British government, and an English-language Bible
could not be printed without a special license from
the British government; all English-language Bibles
had to bear the imprint of the Crown. However, other
language Bibles were printed in America, including
America's first—the Eliot Bible (1661-1663), by John
Eliot, the "Apostle to the Indians," but his Bible was
in the Massachusetts Indian language. Bibles could
also be printed in French, Spanish, Latin, Greek, other

Indian languages—just about anything but English.

Because English-language Bibles could not be printed in America but had to be imported, when the Revolution began and the British began to blockade all materials coming to America, the ability to obtain such Bibles ended. Therefore, in 1777, America began experiencing a shortage of several important commodities, including Bibles. On July 7, a request was placed before Congress to print or import more because "unless timely care be used to prevent it, we shall not have Bibles for our schools and families and for the public worship of God in our churches." Congress concurred with that assessment and announced: "The Congress desire to have a Bible printed under their care and by their encouragement." A special committee overseeing that project therefore recommended:

> "[T]he use of the Bible is so universal and its importance so great, …your Committee recommend that Congress will order the Committee of Commerce to import 20,000 Bibles from Holland, Scotland, or elsewhere, into the different ports of the States of the Union."[3]

Four years later, in January 1781, Robert Aitken (publisher of the *Pennsylvania Magazine* in Philadelphia) petitioned Congress for permission to print an English-language Bible on his presses in America, rather than import the Bibles. In his memorial to Congress, Aitken said "your Memorialist begs leave to, inform your Honours That he both begun and made considerable progress in a neat Edition of the Holy Scriptures for the use of schools" and went on to say "your Memorialist prays, that he may be commissioned or otherwise appointed and Authorized to print and vend Editions of, the Sacred Scriptures, in such manner and form as may best suit the wants and demands of the good people of these States."

Congress appointed a committee that was to "from time to time [attend] to his progress in the work; that they also [recommend] it to the two Chaplains of Congress to examine and give their opinion of the execution." The committee, comprised of Founding Fathers James Duane, Thomas McKean, and John Witherspoon, reported back to Congress in September 1782 giving its full approval.[4]

Alexis de Tocqueville, a French political scientist and historian who visited the United States extensively in the early 1800s, wrote in his book *Democracy in America*:

"On my arrival in the United States the religious aspect of the country was the first thing that struck my attention; and the longer I stayed there, the more I perceived the great political consequences resulting from this new state of things. In France I had almost always seen the spirit of religion and the spirit of freedom marching in opposite directions. But in America I found they were intimately united and that they reigned in common over the same country."[5]

CAN YOU IMAGINE A WORLD WITHOUT THE BIBLE?

When you realize the foundational role the Bible had in the development of our nation, it's almost impossible to imagine America without it.

I can envision lawless chaos, over-controlling government and overwhelming fear—a world with no morals, values, principles, standards or truth. But you don't have to use your imagination. Just turn on the television news. This is what our youth are encountering on a daily basis in most high schools and universities in our country today.

We have failed our youth—we have not educated them in what they are about to encounter when they leave home and head for college. As a result, they have become victims of humanist, secularist and socialist indoctrination.

We have sent them to war without training them, or without them even knowing they were going to war. As a result, the moral and spiritual casualties are numerous. It's reported that 75 percent of Christians who complete college abandon the faith they possessed when they enrolled. I highly recommend telling your children that they will encounter opposition toward their Christian faith, but they have the right to speak up and stand firm for their beliefs. If they know what to expect, they won't be caught off guard and left wondering what to do.

Abraham Lincoln made this profound statement: "The philosophy of the school room in one generation will be the philosophy of government in the next."[6] Is it any wonder that our government is as unqualified and dysfunctional as it has become? Simply look at how many of our professional politicians (who were elected to be public *servants*) have been educated in our public school system, and that reveals the answer.

Due to uninformed voting—or by not voting at all—citizens are now required to live with what we have allowed. We are suffering the consequences of years of historical ignorance, which leads to irresponsibility. What we are now forced to live with is not what most of us desire. How long we live this dysfunctional lifestyle is up to us.

We as a nation no longer know our national history, or Bible history, and as a result we have lost our direction and forgotten our purpose. Many young citizens no longer know how to protect the legal rights that

God has blessed them with. Like Israel, we have forgotten the great and mighty things that God has done for us; as a result, we are witnessing the consequences.

The question now, as it was in the Old Testament stories, is, *Can our failure to protect what God has given us be reversed?* The answer is emphatically, *yes*—if we will remember what we have forgotten.

When history is ignored, forgotten or revised, we lose our direction, don't know what is correct, and are open to deception, therefore forfeiting our protection.

There is still time to learn our history and recover the wisdom of our past. There is still time to revisit the path of God's desired destiny for us. This will require time and effort if we wish to retain the life God has so graciously blessed us with.

We have a choice. We can invest a tithe of our time and keep all of our freedom. Or we can remain passive, which will demand all of our time and all of our freedom!

Proverbs 11:11 reads: *By the blessing of the influence of the upright and God's favor [because of them] the city is exalted, but it is overthrown by the mouth of the wicked.* Notice that this verse does not say, "by the blessing of the upright the city is exalted." It reveals that the city is exalted due to God's favor because the upright were influential. It also reveals that the city is overthrown when the upright are lacking in influence.

This means there is no resistance to evil. When Christians are not influential, they leave a void that will be filled with evil activism.

The rest of this story is yet to be written. God is waiting for us to fulfill our part. Our destiny hangs in the balance.

CHAPTER 6

The False Promises of Socialism and Communism

"We can't expect the American people to jump
from capitalism to communism but we can
assist their elected leaders in giving them
small doses of socialism until one day they
will awaken to find they have communism."[1]
—attributed to Nikita Khrushchev,
Soviet Union Premier from 1958 to 1964

*Nevertheless, the people refused to listen
to the voice of Samuel, and they said, No!
We will have a king over us.*
—1 Samuel 8:19

When I was in my teens, 20s and 30s and beyond, the words socialism and communism were almost like curse words in terms of political philosophy.

This was during the Cold War—from the 1940s to the early 1990s—a time when the United States and the communist Soviet Union were in a posture of war but were not engaged in actual military conflict. Because the Soviet Union and the United States possessed nuclear weapons and threats were common between the two countries, schools would often perform safety drills in school to prepare for an enemy attack. My classmates and I would crawl under our desks when an alarm sounded. And after a minute or two, when the siren stopped, we'd go back to sitting at our desks.

I'm not sure how our desks would have protected us from the blast of an atomic bomb, but that was the routine. And the fear it instilled was real. We were told all-out nuclear war could erupt at a moment's notice, and I suppose this may have influenced my decision to join the Army.

During some of the most contentious days of the Cold War, I was stationed in what was then referred to as West Germany. After World War II, the country was divided in two, with the eastern side controlled by the Soviet Union, who installed puppet leaders under their communist regime. The separating line between East and West Germany was the famous Berlin Wall.

NIGHT AND DAY

This physical and political wall created two distinct Germanys, with stark differences for its citizens. The communist-controlled East Germany had a government-run economy and a much lower standard of living than the democratic, free-market West Germany. (The same was true for the other Soviet-controlled countries in Eastern Europe, like Poland.)

In just 30 years after the wall was established, the differences between these two nations became as stark as night and day. On the communist side of the wall, people lived in fear and did not even have the freedom to speak out against the government. Those who dared to cross over from East to West were hunted down and often shot by the communist border guards. Yes, the government killed their own citizens for the "crime" of trying to escape. Their economy was almost Third World, compared to the thriving economy of the West.

After the wall was removed in 1989, tens of thousands of East Germans flooded into West Germany and were astounded at the standard of living their countrymen enjoyed. It was extreme culture shock.

Inspired by the bravery of freedom-loving people in Germany and Poland, citizens of other communist-controlled countries in the area also rose up and claimed independence from the Soviet Union. Many of the uprisings were led by prominent Christians and supported by church leaders. These nations have been on the road to prosperity and freedom ever since.

Joyce and I, along with our ministry team, have

had the honor of ministering in Albania and Poland, and our television broadcast is televised in these and other former communist countries. This would have been illegal in the time when communism ruled.

The ultimate goal of communism and socialism is to remove God from the lives of people. Why? Because faith in God stands in the way of people placing their faith in government. The Word of God puts restrictions on government and therefore puts limits on their power.

In socialism and communism—which are basically the same—government seeks to become a god.

When I worked in the engineering field, one of my coworkers was from Russia, and he had many fascinating stories about life in the former Soviet Union. Citizens had to obtain approval for every major decision. There were restrictions on cars, housing and even food. Just imagine not being able to move from one apartment to another without getting government approval, and often that approval is not given.

Joyce buys a lot of her clothes from a boutique owned and operated by a woman from Poland. This woman has talked about how shocked she is by the attitude of many Americans toward their freedom and the opportunity we have to work hard and succeed in life. She and her family came here with almost nothing and now she owns several clothing businesses. She's very grateful for the freedom she enjoys in the United States—and is thankful, because she has lived without freedom. But we often fail to be thankful because we take our freedom for granted. It is something we have always had and don't think about the importance of it or the need to protect it.

Yes, where she lived in communist Poland they were guaranteed housing and food, but lived without freedom. She realizes what a blessing freedom is.

Socialism and communism promise the moon to people, but in actual fact they deliver gloom. Today's example of communism in action, and the resulting destruction of freedom, is what we now see in the South American country of Venezuela.

This was a relatively prosperous country until a communist leader rose to power with false promises. In just a few years, Venezuela has declined into extreme poverty and civil war, despite the fact that it's one of the most oil-rich nations on earth. More than 5 million people have fled to escape the conditions now present in this country.

The promise of socialism and communism is tempting. Karl Marx said, "From each according to his ability, to each according to his needs!"[2] For many, this arrangement sounds like the answer to all their problems. But what Marx never explains was exactly *how* the money, food and possessions would be acquired.

FORTY PERCENT

Today, according to a 2019 Gallup Poll, four in 10 Americans embrace some form of socialism.[3] In less than 50 years, socialism has transitioned from a bad word to a popular campaign slogan. How did this shift happen?

People were deceived because of a lack of knowledge. Because they didn't have a clear understanding of our history, they were unable to perceive and respond to the warnings.

In 1 Samuel 8:6-20, the prophet Samuel warned the people about putting their faith in an earthly government to take care of them. As you read the verses below, think about the parallels of today's political philosophies.

> But it displeased Samuel when they said, Give us a king to govern us. And Samuel prayed to the Lord. And the Lord said to Samuel, Hearken to the voice of the people in all they say to you; for they have not rejected you, but they have rejected Me, that I should not be King over them.
>
> According to all the works which they have done since I brought them up out of Egypt even to this day, forsaking Me and serving other gods, so they also do to you. So listen now to their voice; only solemnly warn them and show them the ways of the king who shall reign over them.

So Samuel told all the words of the Lord to the people who asked of him a king. And he said, These will be the ways of the king who shall reign over you: he will take your sons and appoint them to his chariots and to be his horsemen and to run before his chariots. He will appoint them for himself to be commanders over thousands and over fifties, and some to plow his ground and to reap his harvest and to make his implements of war and equipment for his chariots. He will take your daughters to be perfumers, cooks, and bakers.

He will take your fields, your vineyards, and your olive orchards, even the best of them, and give them to his servants. He will take a tenth of your grain and of your vineyards and give it to his officers and to his servants. He will take your men and women servants and the best of your cattle and your donkeys and put them to his work.

He will take a tenth of your flocks, and you yourselves shall be his slaves. In that day you will cry out because of your king you have chosen for yourselves, but the Lord will not hear you then.

Nevertheless, the people refused to listen to the voice of Samuel, and they said, No! We will have a king over us, that we also may be like all the nations, and that our king may govern us and go out before us and fight our battles.

People who believe the government will take care of all their problems will always be bitterly disappointed and ultimately enslaved. Just as the above passage warns: "You yourselves shall be his slaves."

Remember, many of the recently delivered Israelites cried out to go back to slavery in Egypt. They whined about the manna God supernaturally provided for them and longed for the food they had in Egypt (See Numbers 11 and 14).

Those who are ignorant about how government works will fall for false promises.

Those who are ignorant of economics will believe that there's such a thing as "free" money.

Those who are ignorant of history will believe socialism is a better system than capitalism.

Those who are ignorant of how charity works will believe socialism is a "Christian" model of helping the poor.

It is reported that Joseph Stalin, Soviet dictator from 1920 to 1953, said, "America is like a healthy body and its resistance is threefold: its patriotism, its morality and its spiritual life. If we can undermine these three areas, America will collapse from within."[4]

Today, sadly, we can see a decline in patriotism, morality and spiritual life. And we see a rise in the number of Americans who embrace the concept of socialism.

CAPITALISM

Capitalism is not a perfect economic system—no earthly system is perfect—but can you point to a better one? Can you show me a model that fosters more opportunity and prosperity?

To me, capitalism and the concept of free enterprise are simple: a person sees a need, works to develop a way to meet that need, and is then blessed by the value the solution provides. This is a Godly principle: Do unto others as you would have them do unto you (see Matthew 7:12).

Free enterprise allows people to create goods and services that bless others. And then others can freely choose to engage in business with any provider of those solutions at any time.

Socialism and communism are based on people *taking*. Stealing. It's a manifestation of evil.

Those who champion the philosophy of taking don't realize how stealing the life of others can never truly fulfill their own lives. It can only sustain their misery. They don't realize that possessions and false love can never replace God's love. They are motivated by deception and therefore can only operate in an atmosphere of ignorance.

How does a Christian nation become a radical socialistic nation? By allowing the removal of the knowledge of God—systematically—from its history, and then society, because of a lack of resistance.

When believers do not fulfill their Christian civic responsibilities, a spiritual vacuum is created. When God and Godliness disappear from a Christian nation, bondage replaces freedom and what was once normal is replaced by the radical.

J. Edgar Hoover, former director of the Federal Bureau of Investigation, said, "We must now face the harsh truth that the objectives of communism are being steadily advanced because many of us do not recognize the means used to advance them. ... The individual is handicapped by coming face to face with a Conspiracy so monstrous he cannot believe it exists. The American mind simply has not come to a realization of the evil which has been introduced into our midst."[5]

Not doing what needs to be done in the face of evil encourages its existence and growth. Evil is denied existence by wise action, but it abounds because of ignorant silence or laziness.

Silence is a result of people not knowing what to do (historical ignorance). Laziness occurs when people know what to do and choose not to (indifference). Both are forms of irresponsibility with the same outcome: loss of rights and, therefore, loss of freedom.

As Americans, as Christians, and as those who care about the quality of life for our fellow citizens, we must not be silent or passive.

The Bible makes it clear that government is not the answer. History clearly shows that communism and socialism only deliver depression and poverty. But those who oppose God and freedom are patient and crafty. Liberalism says we need government to grow. And socialism says we need government in control.

Free markets—and free people—are a threat to this agenda.

Let me be clear. I'm not saying those who promote socialism are evil. Many believe they are acting out of compassion and love. But they are ignorant of the truth.

SOCIALISM SPREADS SLOWLY

Norman Thomas, long-time leader in the Socialist Party in the United States and a six-time candidate for president, is often quoted as saying, "The American people will never knowingly adopt Socialism, but under the name of 'liberalism' they will adopt every fragment of the Socialist program, until one day America will be a socialist nation without knowing how it happened."[6]

That statement was reportedly made over 70 years ago and must have seemed like an impossibility to most Americans. Yet today, a large part of the Body of Christ has become complacent in regard to socialism instead of confronting this destroyer of freedom and prosperity.

Around the same time, Russian-American novelist Ayn Rand wrote, "We are fast approaching the stage of the ultimate inversion: the stage where the government is free to do anything it pleases, while the citizens may act only by permission; which is the stage of the darkest periods of human history, the stage of rule by brute force."[7]

Foresight through hindsight produces insight.

Unless the people of this nation recognize the storm flags waving, we are doomed to repeat the past mistakes of those who refused to pay attention to history. We have the knowledge and time to make a course correction.

Freedom is costly but priceless. It comes at a high cost and remains only with high maintenance. The freedom we have, if not maintained, will not remain. And if it's lost because we failed to pay the cost, we'll realize too late we've created our own fate.

CHAPTER 7

Faith in Action

"...Under the old system the question
was *how* to read the Constitution.
Under the new approach, the question
is *whether* to read the Constitution."[1]
—Former U.S. Attorney General Edwin Meese III

*What does it profit, my brethren, if someone says
he has faith but does not have works? Can faith
save him? If a brother or sister is naked and destitute of daily food, and one of you says to them,
"Depart in peace, be warmed and filled," but you
do not give them the things which are needed for
the body, what does it profit? Thus also faith by
itself, if it does not have works, is dead.*
—James 2:14-17 (NKJV)

Meditation in God's Word reveals God's ways, gives
revelation of God's will, creates inspiration in our lives,

and causes motivation, which produces activation of the manifestation of our destination for His glorification.

As I have read the true history of our country and about the many Founders who were involved in shaping and establishing this great nation—a nation we have been given the privilege to live in—it's very evident that the statement above describes nearly all of their lives.

From this description, which begins with meditation in God's Word and ends with His glorification, we see the process of our Founders' exceptional walk with God. What we don't see is their daily responsibilities, which they were required—and now we are required—to fulfill. These responsibilities are made clear in the Word of God and were fulfilled by those dedicated citizens who went before us. It created prosperity, and, as a nation, they dealt wisely and enjoyed success (see Joshua 1:8).

Voting for principled candidates—and praying for those candidates and our country—is very important, but that's not where our responsibilities stop. Our Founding Fathers taught and lived eternal vigilance. My definition of eternal vigilance is *constant diligence in excellence.*

They fulfilled their Christian civic responsibilities as a natural part of their responsibility to their country and their God. They did so because that is what they were taught to do in their homes, churches and schools. As a result, their diligence in excellence became our inheritance. The question now is: What inheritance will we leave our children and grandchildren as a result of our diligence or lack thereof? Will their inheritance inspire them to bless us? What we do with our portion of history will make all the difference in our destiny— and their inheritance.

STEPS TO RIGHT ACTIONS

Right actions begin with remembrance. When Israel forgot all the great and mighty miracles God had performed in their lives, that's when they went into bondage. When they did remember, they repented, became responsible, and were restored.

People in this country, including Christians, are not nearly as excited about the right to vote as they once were, and fewer still are engaged in holding their elected leaders accountable. The same is true of prayer rallies and other event-driven actions. Yes, we need to gather and pray, but this is a starting point, not the end of our involvement. Often, people pray with no intention of taking action; they want God to fulfill their responsibility.

Informed involvement requires us to invest in increasing our knowledge. If people aren't knowledgeable, they have no ability to elect the right people and hold them responsible to represent them.

Because of a lack of knowledge, most people vote for candidates who make promises but have no principles. Then, when those promises aren't fulfilled, all they do is complain. This is what happens when leaders who make promises, but lack character, are elected by uninformed, emotionally driven voters.

If more Christians voted for principled candidates and then expressed their concerns and ideas to their elected leaders, we would see positive results. And if we would offer support and encouragement to Godly leaders who stand for what is right, we would encourage them to continue making right decisions in the future.

It's not only important to speak with elected officials, but we should also speak with our friends and neighbors about matters that are important to us. Too many Christians feel intimidated about political involvement of any kind—including voting! Christians are nervous about speaking up because they lack knowledge about the issues (like how our founding principles have been abandoned) and don't understand their rights. Our simple encouragement, and sharing the knowledge we have about issues, will give others confidence.

The bottom line is taking responsibility—based on knowledge, remembrance and repentance. Only then will we experience revival and restoration.

Not being knowledgeable produces anger and

frustration because nothing ever changes; but action based on knowledge produces restoration, positive change, and joy.

THE CRUCIAL ACTION OF SPEAKING UP

In the last 50 years, there have been few issues of law more hotly contested or misunderstood than the First Amendment. What began as a safeguard for religious freedom is now actually being used to *remove* expressions of the Christian faith from the public arena. Forbidding prayer at a school assembly or preventing crosses from being displayed at roadside memorials and military gravesites are just two examples.

As we discussed in Chapter 2, at the heart of the issue are the now-famous words, "separation of church and state." Through continual usage over recent decades, the "separation" language has become so commonplace that many Americans believe it to be a constitutional phrase found in the First Amendment. *But it is not.* Here's what the First Amendment actually says:

> "Congress shall make no laws respecting an establishment of religion, or prohibiting the free exercise thereof...."[2]

Contrary to what many believe, the phrase "separation of church and state" never even appears in the

First Amendment, anywhere in the Constitution, or in any of our founding documents. However, with these misleading five words as the standard, the courts have now declared many American customs and traditions unconstitutional.

Because of this false interpretation, the Ten Commandments, prayer, and Bible reading have all been removed from public schools. It all began in 1801, many years after the Constitution was ratified, when President Thomas Jefferson received a letter from the Baptist Association of Danbury, Connecticut. This group was strongly in favor of the First Amendment; however, they were worried the government could one day attempt to regulate religious expression. They were afraid the language in the amendment *wasn't strong enough*.

Specifically, there was concern about the establishment of a national church, such as the Church of England. The Baptists wanted to secure their freedom and assure the government could not interfere with the religious activities of its citizens or show partiality to any one denomination. On January 1, 1802, Jefferson wrote a reassuring reply to the Danbury Baptists. In it, he said:

"...Believing with you that religion is a matter which lies solely between man and his God; that he owes account to none other for his faith or his worship...I contemplate with solemn reverence that the act of the whole American people which declared that their legislature should 'make no law respecting an establishment of religion or prohibiting the free exercise thereof,' thus building a wall of separation between Church and State...I shall see with sincere satisfaction the progress of those sentiments which tend to restore to man all his natural rights...."[3]

The use of the term "natural rights" is extremely important. While this term doesn't mean much to us now, it spoke volumes to the people in that day. "Natural rights" was understood to include everything God has promised within His holy Scriptures. Therefore, the Danbury Baptists were assured by Jefferson that freedom of religion was an inalienable *God-given right* and above federal jurisdiction.

The "wall" in his Danbury letter was not intended to restrict religious displays in public. Instead, it was to *minimize* the power of the government to prohibit or interfere with religious expression.

Jefferson confirmed an important fact: The First Amendment is not meant to protect government from religion—it is to protect religion and churches from the government![4]

If we don't know our *true* Godly history and what is ours, then we won't recognize when these freedoms are taken away.

THE TRAGEDY OF INACTION

In 1962, the Supreme Court took prayer out of public schools. In 1963, they then prohibited these same schools from having Bibles in their classrooms. Combined with the 1947 decision that redefined the First Amendment and demanded a "separation of church and state," these new laws branched into every area, slowly erasing common expressions of reverence for God from American society.

Simultaneously, the recent teaching of moral relativism in our universities—rejecting the cultural and moral values of our past—had also reached a tipping point, leading to increased drug use, immorality, declining church attendance, and anti-American sentiment among our nation's youth.

Together, these forces created one of the greatest societal shifts in American history. Here are a few examples:

- In 1962, the birth rate for unwed teenagers (ages 15-19) was at a decade low before rising sharply to a 50% increase in 1970, on its way to a 200% increase in 1993.[5]
- From 1951 to 1962, the annual number of violent crimes in America rose from 160,000 to 250,000. However, 1962 signaled an abrupt shift, with violent crimes rising to 750,000 in 1972, on its way to 1.9 million in 1993.[6]

- In 1963, the average SAT exam score was 980, the highest it had been in more than a decade. It then significantly dropped each year after—plummeting to 920 in 1974, eventually down to 890 in 1980.[7]

Certainly, there are occasions when governments do need to change and make social adjustments. However, Article V of the Constitution clearly defines that these changes should originate *from the people*. It establishes the proper way for us to adjust or "evolve" our government through Congress and legislation—*not* through independent revisions by the Supreme Court.[8]

When the Supreme Court chose to evolve society through taking prayer and the Bible out of schools, it was more than a revision of our Constitution—*it was also contrary to the will of the people*. National polls taken by Gallup and other large news organizations show that three-fourths of the nation still approved of voluntary school prayer years after the decision was turned into law.[9]

Maybe worst of all, most Americans had no knowledge of these changes until it was too late. They were ignorant, and therefore did not speak up.

This is a special time in history. America is at a crossroads, and the direction it takes is up to us. I believe we *can* begin to take back what has been lost, but it's going to require understanding our responsibilities and taking action. I encourage you to:

- Participate in civil government as opportunities allow.
- Vote for Godly leaders who want to protect our Constitution.
- Contact your representatives to promote policies that are constitutional.
- Pray for God to change the hearts of our leaders and the American people.
- Inform your elected representatives that you want them to reinstate our true Godly heritage into the history books of the high schools and colleges of our nation.

Will you join me in taking God-inspired action?

As I write this, I recently celebrated my 80th birthday. I remember an America that was very different. Less fear. Less hopelessness. As a young teenager, I had a newspaper route. For those too young to know what that is, I was paid to get up very early and deliver newspapers in my neighborhood for very little money.

I rode my bike around by myself and never even thought about my personal safety. I vividly remember a news story about a paperboy who was robbed. It was front-page news that shocked me and stunned the community. In the section where I grew up in my city, everybody knew everybody and walked around in peace and safety. It wasn't even necessary to keep the doors of our homes locked during the night.

Today our communities are isolated and gated. Because we didn't fulfill our responsibilities, we lost our freedoms. When freedom is lost, security is lost. Let's not be deceived into trading freedom for so-called security.

VOTING IS ACTION

When unprincipled candidates who make unrealistic promises are elected by uninformed voters, an unqualified, dysfunctional government is the result.

Whenever there is a lack of knowledge, there is an abundance of deception masquerading as truth. Which is more dangerous: politicians with wrong motives, or uniformed Christians who elect such people as their leaders?

Nations are not destroyed because bad people do wrong, but because good people fail to do right. Evil is denied existence by wise action, but it abounds because of ignorant silence and laziness.

We as individuals and as a nation will be held accountable for our lack of action when action is required. We will also be held accountable for wrong action when right action is required. Many Christians think their lack of responsibility is not a problem because "God is in control." What they don't realize is God is not in control of their responsibility.

God will not vindicate the irresponsible because of ignorance, and we cannot hide our incompetence behind our religiosity and think we are unaccountable.

Not voting is a great example of lack of action when action is required. Voting for unprincipled candidates who make unrealistic promises is a case of wrong action when right action is required. Voting is the greatest privilege and responsibility of any free nation. The future freedom of a nation is dependent upon the actions of its citizens.

Thomas Jefferson, our nation's third president, made this statement, "If we can but prevent the government from wasting the labors of the people under the pretense of taking care of them, they must become happy."[10]

When a Christian constitutional republic deteriorates to a socialistic government, it's because Christians have failed to fulfill their civic responsibilities by not taking action.

GOD ASKS FOR OUR ACTION

Scripture is filled with countless examples of God asking believers to take action *before* He takes corresponding action. Before Jesus raised Lazarus from the dead, He asked those gathered to roll away the stone. As Joyce has pointed out in her teachings, it certainly took miraculous power to raise a person from the dead; so why did Jesus tell the people to remove the stone? (See John 11:38-41.) Why didn't He just do it Himself?

God is sovereign and can do anything He chooses to do, but He normally works in partnership with His children. He uses our faith and God-inspired action. If the stone is never rolled away, the miracle is never seen. Rolling the stone away is our responsibility; the miracle of restoration is God's responsibility. If we do not fulfill our responsibility, God will not perform the miracles we pray for. In obedience to God, we must do the *possible* if we want to see God do the *impossible*.

Peter had to get out of the boat before he could walk on the water (see Matthew 14:22-33). The priests carrying the ark of the covenant had to put their feet in the Jordan River before the waters parted for the Israelites to cross over safely (see Joshua 3:13). Moses had to stretch out his rod over the Red Sea before God parted the waters (see Exodus 14:16). The servants had to fill the pots with water before Jesus turned the water into wine (see John 2:7).

TIMIDITY VS. TENACITY

Each one of us is faced with a choice: Will we live with the vitality of tenacity or the passivity of timidity?

God does not bless timidity. God blesses *tenacity*.

Timidity is the lack of response, due to ignorance, which produces cowardice. A timid person or nation will run, hide or compromise when courage is required. They will forfeit their rights without resistance when threatened by bullies. A timid person or nation will eventually become the slave of the intimidator.

Tenacity, on the other hand, leads to courageous response due to having correct knowledge. A tenacious person or nation runs to the battle. They are always ready to fight for their rights if that is what is required. A tenacious person or nation would rather die fighting for freedom than live as a slave.

This is why Patrick Henry, one of our Founding Fathers, made this statement during the Revolutionary War, one of the most critical times in our nation's history: *"Give me liberty or give me death."*

Courage will never yield when fear sends the invitation to compromise.

Courage is the willingness and ability to risk who you are and what you have for what you want and who you want to become.

Courage is the highest expression of responsibility, but it cannot function in an atmosphere of ignorance. Without knowledge, it has no platform.

America's courage has been made dormant due to ignorance through the revision of her history.

First Samuel 17 teaches us a vital lesson about courage. King Saul and all of Israel were intimidated by Goliath. However, David courageously ran at Goliath and slew the intimidator.

The Bible tells us that God has not given us the spirit of timidity, but He has given us a spirit of power, love and a sound mind (see 2 Timothy 1:7).

Timidity becomes passive power through ignorance. Tenacity is the activity of aggressive power through correct knowledge.

ACTION PREVENTS INJUSTICE

Immediate and just action prevents future unjust aggression. When a one-time event, instead of a movement, is our answer to injustice, then injustice is guaranteed its goal. It is futile to expose and threaten injustice without penalizing it. If injustice is not killed in its infancy, it will persist and grow stronger. And the stronger it becomes, the harder it is to get rid of.

When frustration replaces motivated action, justice cannot be served!

The Revolutionary War is the perfect example. This war was a results-motivated *action* instead of frustrated *reaction*. It was a movement (a revolution) to prevent the loss of freedom and the eventual enslavement of the colonies, which would have meant British rule and no U.S.A.

The required price for this freedom was the possible death of all who opposed the British. The colonists understood the cost of freedom and were willing to pay the ultimate price. We can thank God they were willing to pay that price!

The price for the prize of freedom is eternal vigilance, whatever the cost. The cause for the loss of freedom is temporary negligence, which promotes passive resistance to unjust actions.

Because of their courage, the colonists became the beneficiaries of that freedom, and we have become the eventual inheritors. However, if the colonists would have opposed the British through frustration and complaining—instead of continual, responsible action—the United States would not exist today.

A movement is birthed from motivation, and it requires constant action, at whatever the cost, to attain the necessary solution. However, an event is temporary noise without required action. It is birthed out of frustration and will never prevent eventual devastation.

Today, there are many events—we may see people show up once or twice to oppose something. However, results only come from organized, persistent efforts. If we want victory—if we want to preserve the rights and freedoms we've been given—it is going to require us to be relentless. We need to refuse to give up until we see results!

When prayer was taken out of schools, there were a few people who briefly objected. But there was no organized effort to stop it from happening. The moral majority was very large, but the response was small. Because of a lack of action, we settled for this great injustice and now we're forced to live with the consequences.

When we don't learn from history, we forfeit the wisdom that reveals our responsibilities. History repeats itself and the cost is the systematic dismantling of our inheritance.

EXAMPLES OF CHRISTIAN CIVICS IN ACTION

To show what Christian civic involvement can look like, here are some stories from our friend David Barton, the founder of WallBuilders. WallBuilders is an organization dedicated to educating people about America's forgotten history and the moral, religious and constitutional foundation upon which this nation was built. David is also the author of several excellent books, which we reference in the appendix.

There are numerous instances in which we have seen individuals make a substantial difference by doing what are often easy things. They simply took action when no one else did, or when no one else had thought of doing so. The result changed their communities, and sometimes much more.

One example is Bruce Barilla of West Virginia. A grandson of Russian and Polish immigrants, he made his living as a janitor at a small local college. He saw that a regular part of life in America was commemorative weeks, such as Free Speech Week, National Postcard Week, Parkinson's Awareness Week, and so forth. He wondered why there was no Christian Heritage Week so he wrote to his governor and asked him to proclaim one—which the governor did. Bruce then wrote other governors, asking them to do the same—a practice he has continued for years. As a result of these simple letters, over 700 Christian Heritage Week proclamations have been issued in dozens of states across the nation. (To see these proclamations, or to ask your governor or mayor to issue one, visit wallbuilders.com/chw.)

In a similar story, Jacquie Sullivan is a grandmother who serves on the city council of Bakersfield, California. She asked her fellow council members to make the national motto, "In God We Trust," the Bakersfield city motto. They voted, and her motion passed. They then publicly posted the motto in the city council chambers. Jacquie began contacting local cities and counties, asking them to do the same, and now over 700 cities and counties in dozens of states prominently display "In God We Trust" in their official chambers. (You can ask your city or county officials to do the same. For information, visit InGodWeTrustAmerica.org.)

Others have been inspired by Jacquie's actions and expanded them into new areas. For example, a number of state legislatures have passed laws requiring that "In God We Trust" be displayed in every classroom in the state (including Arkansas, Florida, Louisiana, Mississippi, Tennessee, Utah and Virginia). States such as Indiana, Pennsylvania, Utah, Tennessee and West Virginia have added "In God We Trust" to their license plates. And many local police and sheriff departments now place the national motto on each of their vehicles. Additionally, over 3 million homes, businesses and individuals now proudly display individual decals of the phrase. (For more information, visit InGodWeTrustAmerica.org.)

Some may dismiss these actions as trivial or inconsequential, but they are not. When Americans are God-conscious, it makes a big difference in their behavior. As the Bible affirms in Romans 1:28, *...As they did not see fit to acknowledge God, God gave them up to a depraved mind, to do those things that are not proper* (NASB). Once people stop being God-conscious, their behavior changes, the culture coarsens, and they begin doing those things "that are not proper."

Proverbs 3:5-6 reemphasizes the pivotal message that in all our ways (including public life) we are to acknowledge Him. Psalm 79:6 and Jeremiah 10:25 call for God's wrath upon all nations that do not call upon His name. And Matthew 10:32 and Luke 12:8 affirm the blessings of acknowledging Him in public. The warranty of 1 Samuel 2:30 (NIV) that *Those who honor me I will honor, but those who despise me will be disdained*, applies to nations as well as individuals. The biblical message is clear: It is essential to acknowledge and honor God publicly.

While individuals such as Bruce and Jacquie started local movements that grew to the national level, other Christians decided to impact the culture by focusing on local policies. After all, God blesses or punishes a people based on their public policies (see Proverbs 14:34).

One example of an individual who wanted to change local politics is that of an elderly pastor from a small community church in San Antonio. The local school district had 5,000 students, and when the pastor learned of corruption on the school board, he decided to act. He began recruiting good candidates to run. When election night came, all of the incumbents were decisively defeated, and the candidates he recruited received from 62% to 71% of the vote. They included a minister, a youth pastor, a deacon, and a Bible study teacher. That school district was put on a new path because the elderly pastor of a small church decided to act.

Sadly, Americans too often view all elections through the lens of national races, so local elections such as school board and city council are often neglected or ignored. Consequently, there was "only 5% voter turnout in a recent Dallas mayoral election. Six percent in Charlotte, 7.5% in San Antonio. Seven percent in Austin. Seven percent in Tennessee's congressional primaries, 6% for a statewide gubernatorial primary in Kentucky, 3% for a U.S. Senate primary in Texas, and 3% for a statewide runoff in North Carolina."[11]

Typical of these numbers, Eric Garcetti was a candidate in a city election that involved over 40 debates and more than $19 million spent on advertising. Upon winning and becoming mayor of Los Angeles, he reported, "I got 33% of the 20% turnout of the 49% of the population registered to vote. I had a landslide with 2.6% of the population."[12]

With such poor local turnout, it is possible for Christians to have a substantial impact, if they will just engage.

Consider, for example, Fort Worth, Texas, a city of just under 1 million citizens. Its school board was the first in the nation to announce (in July 2016) that student genders would no longer be recognized—that boys and girls would share the same bathrooms and locker facilities. The president of the United States at that time then took that Fort Worth policy and implemented it nationally through the U.S. Department of Education. There was a strong local outcry against the policy, but little happened afterward. However, it could have been different, just as it had been in San Antonio.

After all, the president of the school board had received less than 900 votes (and there were over 23,000 voters in his district). Yet, there was an evangelical church near him with over 3,000 adults, which represented many times more votes than he received in his election. That one church could have solved the problem. It would have been equally easy to replace the rest of the board if anyone had taken action, but no one did. Too many churches and Christians across the country have failed to engage in influencing and shaping their local communities.

But it's not just big cities that have abysmal turnout; the same problem plagues smaller communities. For example, in a northeast Iowa community of 500 citizens, a farmer decided to run for school board. On election day, he got busy and failed to vote, and he lost—because no one voted in the election! If he had just voted for himself, he would have been on the school board!

In northwest Arkansas, a Christian woman decided to run for the school board to prevent bad policies (like those in Fort Worth) from being implemented. In a town of 50,000 citizens, she received only 35 total votes—and won.

Years ago I personally learned that one church can shift an entire community. Our town had 600 citizens, but its civil government was dysfunctional and corrupt, with various individuals and factions fighting each other within city hall. The city was deep in debt and a half dozen lawsuits (including some by the federal government) had been filed against it for its incompetence and repeated legal violations.

I knew we could do better. I knew that Christians had something to offer. There were four churches in our town, so I met with the pastors, pointed out the problems, and recommended that we recruit candidates from among the churches. Each was to meet the biblical qualifications for civil leaders from Exodus 18:21: ...*honest men who fear God and hate bribes. Appoint them as leaders over groups of one thousand, one hundred, fifty, and ten* (NLT). The pastors agreed. They would come up with candidates the other churches and Christians would get behind.

As election day approached, the other churches had recruited no one, so they told me, "You do it." Our church was small, but we had strong, qualified biblical Christians who agreed to run. The other churches got behind them and all were elected. In only one election, we had a new mayor and city council. Within six months, the city was out of debt and all the lawsuits had been settled. Biblical leaders made the difference, and the city became a pleasant place for all its citizens.

Everyone can and must make a difference in some way.

TAKE A STEP

At this point in the book, I'd like to ask you two important questions. Please take a few moments, consider your answers, and write them down. Then, share them with a loved one or friend.

So far in your reading, which specific areas have stirred you the most? (For example: voting, or a particular issue that you are passionate about.)

What simple action could you take in the arena of those interests? (This might include simple first steps like emailing an elected official or speaking with neighbors or friends at church.)

President James A. Garfield, a Christian minister, articulated this truth when he reminded Americans:

"Now more than ever before, the people are responsible for the character of their Congress. If that body be ignorant, reckless, and corrupt, it is because the people tolerate ignorance, recklessness and corruption."[13]

Knowledge of God creates reliance on God, which creates obedience to God and yields blessings from God.

CHAPTER 8

Restoring Our Education

"Virtue is not hereditary."[1]
— Thomas Paine

*"For I have known him, in order that he may
command his children and his household after him,
that they keep the way of the Lord, to do
righteousness and justice, that the Lord may bring
to Abraham what He has spoken to him."*
—Genesis 18:19 (NKJV)

I graduated from high school in 1958. This was before prayer, and reverence for the Bible, were removed from public schools. There was a freedom to express your faith and share it with others. Today there is opposition.

Every morning we stood and recited the Pledge of Allegiance. Today the pledge is seldom, if ever, recited in the classrooms of our public school system. I believe there are two major reasons why some people in power want the pledge removed: because of the words "under God" and "republic." We are dealing with the removal of God from public education and the deception of our republic being portrayed as a democracy.

Today, at most of the colleges and universities in America, there is an attempt to isolate and intimidate Christians from expressing their faith. They're told—in words and actions—to sit down and shut up. What's the common response to this pressure? More and more Christian students sit down and shut up. Why?

Because they lack courage. Why do they lack courage? Because they lack knowledge of their rights.

Courage cannot function in an atmosphere of ignorance. Courage is the highest expression of responsibility. But without knowledge, courage is paralyzed.

THE IMPORTANCE OF MAINTAINING YOUR DIGNITY

Destroyed history has created a loss of dignity, confused identity and hopeless destiny. The shakedown of the soul of our nation begins with the shakedown of the souls of the people through the revision of their history.

The history of our nation reveals its character—how and why it originated and what it stood for. History reveals the people who were involved, their motives, and what they believed. And it reveals the courage that formed their dignity, displayed their identity and motivated them to fulfill a destiny the world had never seen.

The strength of the people in America originated from their faith in God, which was clearly evident in their rich history. Through this strength, a dignity was developed in their hearts. This dignity revealed their courageous identity to fulfill their desired destiny.

As the true history of America was revised, beginning with the removal of God, it initiated the shakedown of our nation's soul. Without our Godly history, we had no knowledge of who we were and therefore had no platform for our future. Our courage faltered, as it had no ability to function without accurate knowledge of our past.

Since our once vibrant courage became dormant, our responsibility to protect our freedom was silenced. We the people stood by passively, witnessing the shakedown of the soul of our nation. Therefore, many people today are ashamed of themselves because they did not fulfill their responsibility when they had the opportunity. Consequently, they have forfeited their dignity and now exhibit a fearful and hopeless identity.

Your dignity is a representation of who you are, what you stand for and what you believe in. It's the respect and appreciation a person has for themselves. Your dignity is your inner convictions that reveal your identity to yourself and the world.

When a Christian or conservative person takes a stand for what is right and then withdraws their decision because of intimidation (due to ignorance), they become a slave of the intimidator and they forfeit their dignity. As a result, they lose respect for themselves because of their lack of courage to stand for their beliefs. This is why Christians in America are relinquishing their rights. They are intimidated into withdrawing from their convictions.

When moral people are intimidated into forfeiting their dignity to the immoral because of the fear of being ridiculed, courage has been compromised and moral character destroyed.

Dignity is maintained through correct knowledge, resulting in a willingness to take courageous action when faced with critical character decisions; or, dignity is forfeited through the fear of intimidation because of ignorance.

When a person allows others to determine their right and wrong, they have succumbed to dignity theft through intimidation. Their approval status is dictated by what their controllers think, say and allow. They have become victims of intimidation identity slavery.

Intimidation identity slavery is a result of our one-dimensional, politically correct, tolerance-oriented, humanistically programmed and liberally dictated public educational system.

This system dictates what a student is allowed to think and how a student is allowed to act. It tolerates no personal conservative viewpoint. Its goal is the forfeiture of each student's dignity in order to control their identity and ultimately their destiny.

Through our once Godly but now corrupt educational system, we the people are witnessing the shakedown of the soul of our nation.

CHANGING THE FOUNDATIONS OF LEARNING

What is taught in our schools today is a *factual* approach to learning. This might sound perfectly acceptable, but what was taught throughout our history was the *principled* approach—and there is a big difference.

A factual approach teaches the *end result* that "a tree is a tree"—and leaves out *how* a tree became a tree. The process includes a seed, soil, water, sun, an eventual seedling, and time; then you finally end up with a tree. Everything starts with a seed. No seed, no tree. Conception, development and manifestation.

The factual approach teaches a person what's available without teaching the correct method of acquiring it. For instance, when it comes to a car, house, wealth, peace, joy, respect or a successful career, this approach "teaches" that these things are available, but it doesn't instruct a person about the Godly principles required to acquire them.

The principled approach, on the other hand, teaches

conception, process and manifestation (or conclusion). When a person has been educated by the principled approach, their method of acquiring what they desire is to *earn* it. They have learned to earn what they desire.

This includes God's principles of work, effort, time, responsibility, patience, sacrifice and character building.

When a person has been educated in the factual approach, the method of acquiring what they desire can often be to *take*, because they haven't been taught the principles of earning what they desire. This means force, violence, irresponsibility, impatience, theft and character assassination. Our prisons are full of men and women who have applied this method of acquiring what they desire simply because they have not been taught God's principles as the way to live.

The final method of acquiring what one desires is by having things given to them. This often occurs with parents who give their children what they want, with no participation or incentive. Therefore, the children never learn how to be responsible by having to earn what they desire. This means no effort, no work, no responsibility and no character development, but a sense of entitlement.

I learned the following from the book *America's Providential History,* and I offer this summary below:

A "principle," according to Webster's 1828 Dictionary, is: "1. ...the cause, source, or origin of anything;

that from which a thing proceeds; 2. Element; constituent part...."

Briefly stated, the *principle* approach to education instills in individuals the ability to reason from the Bible and apply biblical principles to every aspect of life. As Christians, we know we are supposed to do this, but do we? Do we really know how to reason from the Bible in geography, astronomy, mathematics or history, not to mention national defense or foreign policy?

The principle approach teaches "seed principles" over and over again in each subject and at every grade level, and it includes different illustrations, examples, assignments, educational methods, and more. This ensures that a child not only *knows* biblical principles, but that they *live* them as part of their daily life.

When taught properly, principles are first introduced in seed form to children. God starts with a seed and produces a plant. Today most public schools eliminate principles.[2]

CONVERSION, DIVERSION AND PERVERSION

The fate of America as a republic is deteriorating because of three things: the revised and diluted education system, the distorted and corrupted media, and perverted and polluted entertainment. These three things are destroying the moral character of our people, the innocence of our children, and the beauty of our nation. Will we idly stand by and watch hopelessly as all the blessings God has bestowed on us are taken away? Or will we finally awaken and aggressively take back our rights that are based on Godly principles?

There is no compromising with evil. Evil grows in an atmosphere of ignorance where the spirit of deception has free access. Just as water quenches thirst and food prevents hunger, knowledge dispels ignorance, prevents deception and promotes direction.

It's our time to either shine or allow our light to be put out. God will meet our needs, but He won't fulfill our deeds. Our destiny is in our hands. We will only have ourselves to thank—or blame—for whatever we choose.

There is a major difference between head knowledge and heart knowledge. Heart knowledge reveals the majesty of God, while head knowledge eventually reveals the frailty of mankind. And this difference is determined by our education.

For example, when America's history is taught in most public school classrooms in our nation, God has been removed. Therefore, the factual shape of our history has been disguised so the dysfunctional socialistic agenda can be absorbed by the youth of our nation without any opposition.

For decades, our young people have been, and continue to be, indoctrinated into ignorance as they are fed false facts. Most of them are imprisoned by a faulty worldview—the only worldview they have been allowed to know. Their ability to escape from this prison has been withheld, because the key that could unlock the prison door and set them free has been discarded.

That key can only be found if truth—the majesty of God's grace in America's history—is restored, so that factual *heart* knowledge can expose the deception of distorted *head* knowledge. This is why those who have controlled the public school system have worked so hard to continually control any conservative students or biblical ideas that might expose their radical socialistic agenda.

When America's public education system was created, the government was not involved. It was founded by Christians and it was Bible based.

Benjamin Rush is often referred to as "the father of public schools." He was a signer of the Declaration of Independence, a civic leader, physician, politician, and one of the founders of Dickinson College. Rush said this:

"Without religion, I believe learning does real mischief to the morals and principles of mankind. ... The only means of establishing and perpetuating our republican forms of government is the universal education of our youth in the principles of Christianity by means of the Bible."[3]

In our schools today, they are teaching our young people to turn away from God and turn to "facts." There's a big difference between smart and wise. Smart is head knowledge. Wise is heart knowledge. If you are smart, you may have knowledge about certain subjects but may not know how to *apply* that knowledge. And if you don't have God in your life, and you aren't applying that knowledge with Godly principles, "smart" can become destructive. Knowledge without God can cause a person to be puffed up with pride (see 1 Corinthians 8:1), and that is dangerous because God works through and helps the humble (see 1 Peter 5:6).

In the 1700s, American parents established schools primarily to teach their children the Scriptures. In fact, it was the Christian ministers who originally went house to house, tutoring the students. This was the origin of the first grammar schools.[4]

Did you know 106 of the first 108 colleges were founded on the Christian faith? For example, Harvard was founded by Reverend John Harvard in 1638. Governing rules required the professors to "open and explain the Scriptures to their pupils with integrity and faithfulness."[5]

This is quite a contrast to where we are now! Yes, there are many teachers and administrators who work hard to educate our children with truth and Godly principles, and we honor and are personally grateful for them. However, most of our public schools today teach a worldly, humanistic philosophy that contradicts biblical principles.

The Bible teaches that we reap what we sow (see Galatians 6:7). For centuries, Christianity was *sown* into the hearts of Americans, and we *reaped* growth in liberty and prosperity. In 1962, one persistent person got prayer removed from public schools. Just imagine then what we can do if Christians unite to vote, participate in government, and individually and collectively stand up for our faith.

RESTORING OUR EDUCATIONAL FOUNDATION

I'd like to share some insights from our friend Carole Adams, president of the Foundation for American Christian Education (FACE):

> The Foundation for American Christian Education (www.FACE.net) is a 56-year-old mission to reform American Christian education to its authentic philosophy and methods that built the nation. That authentic teaching and learning process was derailed by the public/government schooling movement in the late 19th and early 20th centuries. It was separated from the influence of the home and the church by the "enlightened elite" universities and teacher colleges.

In the 1940s and '50s, the prescient founders of FACE, Verna Hall and Rosalie Slater, documented the trajectory of American liberty and culture, based upon the left turn taken in the '20s and '30s. The result is these two volumes:

1. *The Christian History of the Constitution of the United States of America: Christian Self-government* by Verna M. Hall, 1960. This volume of primary sources carries the ideals and principles—the way Americans must reason and believe to sustain a self-governing republic—in the words of those who formed it.

2. *Teaching and Learning America's Christian History: the Principle Approach* by Rosalie J. Slater, 1964. This volume contrasts authentic American Christian education to Marxist education—the model Slater observed in the USSR in 1959 at the recommendation of the Stanford professors of her doctoral program. It is a manual for the home, the church and the school. This volume observes that the "traditional" Christian schools of the 1950s and '60s had unknowingly swallowed the methods that produce the character of socialism (in opposition to their very mission). This volume calls Christian educators to take responsibility to form the self-governing character the republic demands—reasoning from

principles and providence that are rooted in natural and moral law.

"The Principle Approach" is the term designating the authentic Christian method of education that formed Christian character and self-government in the early generations of our nation. This approach taught our Founders the principles that structure the U.S. Constitution to protect and empower a self-governing people.

Verna's response was to teach the antidote to the creeping socialism strangling the nation. She uncovered the Christian history of our founding and the Biblical nature of our United States Constitution. Armed with primary documents of our nation's founding, she began to publish and teach the people of our nation.

Verna Hall and co-founder Rosalie Slater tirelessly traveled the country, teaching citizens the truth about America as recorded in our Constitution, Declaration of Independence and the words of statesmen, pastors and teachers. The two spoke to farm bureaus, schools (when able), study groups and in lecture halls. They published the "Red Books," a series of books documenting the biblical nature of our Constitution and Christian founding of our nation. They also published *The Principle Approach*, about the recovery of the biblical method of teaching and learning.

Meanwhile, the ungodly took their message of Marxist ideas to the universities, publicly funded schools and government organizations. They planted the seeds of socialism and communism with the so-called "elite" of the nation.

Today, the contrast of these two philosophies of life and government is very apparent.

The Marxist ideas have matured. We see the harvest from this—destruction of our liberty, property, and institutions and a corruption of our youth.

However, God's providential protection has been upon our nation. FACE is not just a 56-year-old organization, but founders Verna and Rosalie tilled a seedbed for the future of America, raising an army of citizens prepared in biblical Christianity and Christian character to restore our nation. Their work is now evident throughout the nation. A great harvest awaits—citizens who love America and all the ideals it stands for. We continue to teach and publish—to nourish this groundswell of patriots to restore and reinvigorate America!

Today, FACE is establishing a wide network of Principle Approach "demonstration schools" across the country and around the world to model and teach authentic Christian methods of teaching and learning. We encourage, equip and support study groups in churches and local communities. We train (re-train) teachers to replace Marxist philosophies and methods with authentic American Christian practices. We certify Principle Approach master teachers for leadership in schools and communities.

Here is a story from a teacher of one of the Principle Approach demonstration schools:

> We started a small school in Virginia, but I just knew that what we were doing in our little Christian school was not very effective, even though we had the best intentions in the world to practice Christian education. The church was dedicated to it. Huge amounts of resources went into it. We prepared, prepared, prepared. We started a school, and we got into the middle of the year and said, "This doesn't work!"
>
> I had previously taught in a public school at the high school level, but the experience was so negative that I had just shaken the dust off my feet. Our Christian school experience was not producing any better result.
>
> Unplanned by me, but providentially ordered through my pastor and others, I ended up in California visiting a school that supposedly worked well. I was excited to see a Christian school that

my mentors declared, "Works!" However, my pastor had said to me when I was leaving, "While you're there, call the Foundation for American Christian Education (FACE)."

My last day in California, I called the FACE office to ask what they do for Christian schools and what they could do for a small Christian school in Virginia.

At that time, Rosalie (Slater) and Verna (Hall) would both get on the phone extension when someone called. They would often talk over each other, so eager to share wonderful truth. When I asked, "What do you do for Christian schools?" they replied with a question. "What kind of school do you have?"

I told them we had begun an ACE school, as we were told it was an easy way to get started. Without missing a beat, Rosalie June Slater said, "That's too bad, that's too bad." Those words pierced my heart. After working our bones weary for a year, I knew it was "too bad." Without a pause, I asked, "Can I come and see you?" The next morning, we drove 70 miles to San Francisco.

We spent the day at FACE. We were graciously hosted and given a tour of their colonial American collection of artifacts, furniture and books. After lunch, sitting on the couch between Verna and Rosalie, they taught us what authentic Christian education is. It solved so many dilemmas. It opened a vista that was whole and holy and distinctively biblical. It broke through the mass of misinformation about teaching and about education. Suddenly, I saw what teaching could be. Oh my! *This is wonderful!*

I love teaching and I love learning, but it seemed an overwhelming task to prepare as a Principle Approach teacher.

Today, this school is a fully accredited, K-12 educational center with a 40-year history, and it annually reaches the highest average score on the PEERS test. The PEERS test is an assessment tool designed to measure how biblical or non-biblical our thinking is in the major disciplines of life and all areas of culture. It identifies our worldview—the foundational beliefs by which we make choices in life—as it pertains to politics, economics, education, religion, social issues and limited government.

Remember, your children are being formed. Their minds and their hearts are being *formed* by what they do every day. By what they're thinking every day. By how they're spending their time moment by moment. That is what's formative. So, method is key. You need to have something reliable. Some textbooks are reliable, however, not for principles. You won't find biblical foundations there. But with Principle Approach, we go back to the foundation every time. We go back to the principle of understanding God's purpose for our progeny and making sure we're communicating this, along with His covenants and His Word.

How can we prevail in this battle? Knowledge of biblical principles. In the words of Verna Hall:

> "But the blessings of liberty in America cannot be perpetuated unless the principles of that liberty are re-identified and re-affirmed in each generation. This is the role of Christian schools and colleges. America's founding and establishment was the result of a people educated in Christian principles. Only knowledge of these biblical principles can ensure the continuance of them in the civil and religious spheres."

The Christian school—a direct outgrowth of Bible-based Christian churches—has a most critical role to play in restoring Christian leadership to our nation. The anti-Christian education of the progressive state school has produced the socialism and the communism of our times. Teachers are most vital to Christian school education—teachers who are models of Christian character and teachers who are alert to the challenge to America's freedom and the nature of that challenge. Christianity alone is the citadel of America's freedom.

The record of America as a Christian nation resides in the documented history of her founding. This record has been deliberately obscured in order to deprive individuals of their Christian heritage of individual liberty. The rediscovery of the Christian foundation of our country will restore the Christian leadership of America. This knowledge needs to be part of the background of every individual engaged in the education of American youth.

Once the individual becomes informed and aware of the problems of the times, it then becomes critically important to take effective action to correct, reconstruct and rebuild Constitutional liberty. This cannot be accomplished by merely uncovering the problem. With awareness must come constructive knowledge in order to deal intelligently and effectively with every challenge to individual liberty and to the freedom of these United States of America. Human knowledge and human reason are not able to provide the insight and wisdom needed unless one understands the Christian history of this nation and the Christian principles of our form of government.

EDUCATION OR PROGRAMMING?

Following is a story from our friends at Alliance Defending Freedom, an organization that advocates for religious liberty, the sanctity of human life, freedom of speech, and marriage and family. This story is titled: "How one professor's angry censorship backfired."

Nothing. That's what Bernadette Tasy had to show for her pro-life efforts on the Fresno State University campus, as the school year drew to a close.

She and a friend had launched a Students for Life group that fall, gaining only a few non-committal members—and some angry resistance from other students.

Discouragement nagged at Bernadette as she planned one final effort for the school year. For her club's last major activity, she had secured the university's permission to create pro-life chalk messages along the main mall of the campus.

The group had just finished the task when a professor, who taught public health, approached and made it clear he didn't like what they were doing.

Moments later, Bernadette saw a circle of students, enlisted by this professor, smearing out her club's messages with their feet. Stunned, she pulled out her phone to record video of what was happening.

"College campuses are not free speech areas," the

professor snarled as he defaced the messages, claiming that he was exercising his own free speech.

Bernadette walked away shaken but determined to stand up for her rights. Ultimately, she took legal action with the help of Alliance Defending Freedom (ADF). And what the professor meant for harm, God used for good.

Her video confrontation with the professor was posted and went viral, drawing attention to both her case and her pro-life cause. Six months later, her Students for Life group won a resounding victory for free speech on her campus. And, in the middle of it all, they also helped save a life.

"Because something bad happened, and we took the good out of it, and we trusted in God, we were able to take our club further than ever before—to the White House, to saving a student and her baby from abortion, to being a group that other people can look to as a success story—all so that we can intensify the passion that other students have for the pro-life movement," Tasy observed.

"A lot of times when students contact us, they're scared," ADF legal counsel Travis Barham said. "They think, *If I file suit, I'm going to ruin my witness. I'm going to kill my effectiveness on campus. Nobody will want to be part of us. We'll lose members. And this* case is an example of how it could actually be the exact opposite. You could stand up and take action to defend your rights and end up stepping onto a much larger platform where more people can hear what you're trying to say, where more people are drawn to what you're doing—and want to join up with you."

Actually, Bernadette said something very much like this has happened to her:

> "I went from thinking that this pro-life activism experience was just something I would do on the side—if I had time—to feeling that this is my calling, and that I will likely go into full-time pro-life or conservative activism work. And that big change, that big 180, is a product of my experience with Alliance Defending Freedom, Students for Life of America, and all of the other groups that I've been able to meet."

The story above illustrates how knowledge of our rights empowers Christians to take positive action and influence the culture of our education systems.

Without correct education,
there can be no accurate knowledge.

Without accurate knowledge,
there can be no dedication.
Without dedication,
there can be no responsibility.
Without responsibility,
there can be no preservation.
Without preservation,
there can be no rights.
Without rights,
there can be no continuation.
Without continuation,
there can be no freedom.

Do you believe that God cares about our schools and education systems? Of course He does because He cares about every person on the earth and wants them to enjoy life.

The question becomes: What do you believe God wants you to do to improve the educational experience of our children, grandchildren and future generations?

CHAPTER 9

Can a Christian Also Be a Patriot?

"Patriotism: Love of one's country; the passion
which aims to serve one's country, either in
defending it from invasion, or protecting
its rights and maintaining its laws and
institutions in vigor and purity."[1]
—Webster's 1828 Dictionary

*Let every person be loyally subject to the
governing (civil) authorities....*
—Romans 13:1

Can a Christian also be a patriot? My answer to citizens of the United States is: *We cannot sustain this nation without fulfilling our patriotic responsibility.*

Patriotism protects our civil rights, and our civil rights were set up to protect our freedom—including religious freedom.

The quality of our freedom is enhanced or endangered,

depending on whether it is maintained or ignored. The deterioration of every government begins with the decay of the principles on which it was founded, and the decay of the principles results from the lack of responsibility to maintain them.

Patriotism is our responsibility. Everything requires maintenance, whether it's your car, house, body, marriage or country. Everything deteriorates without maintenance—including a society. The quality and life expectancy of anything is greatly enhanced by the care, time and effort invested.

PERSONAL PATRIOTISM

During the writing of this book, I celebrated my 80th birthday. Two days later, my brother celebrated his 81st birthday. He says, "I am 81 going on 99, and my brother Dave is 80 going on 49." The difference is that I've worked out and exercised most of my life and he hasn't. Once in a while, he will make the comment, "I wish I would have done what you have done all these years." And I tell him, "It's too late to change the past, but you can start now!" I'm happy to say he has started to work out and his health has improved.

Patriotism is expressed in the time and effort we are willing to invest to protect the inheritance we've been given as citizens.

In recent years, the word *patriot* has been maligned

by those who want to turn the concept into a negative label. The reason people get away with this—and the reason this word is wrongly perceived—is due to a lack of knowledge concerning our history and the truth of what actually happened in our country.

It's another way to attack our true history...and attempt to do away with God and Godly principles.

Yes, there have been injustices in the United States. However, because of our founding principles, Godly patriots have been able to fight and right many of those wrongs, and we are still working together to continue doing so. In addition, because of free enterprise in our republic, we have greater opportunities to succeed than any other society in history.

Some have tried to say we have a "caste system" in America, which prevents some people from rising in society. Based on decades of our ministry work in India, where the caste system was a part of their culture for hundreds of years, we know quite a bit about the evil of this oppressive system. For example, if your father was a street sweeper, you will be a street sweeper, and your kids will be street sweepers.

In the United States, however, it's possible for anyone to improve their standing in life because of the Godly foundation of our nation. Some who paint America as an unjust country have benefited from our freedoms, but they have failed to appreciate and take advantage of the opportunities in front of them.

Patriotism isn't a love of the policies, culture or laws of 200 years ago. It's a belief in the founding principles that are biblical principles: life, liberty and the pursuit of happiness. Godly principles provide freedom, joy and peace. That's why we respect our flag, because it's ultimately a symbol of liberty and justice for all.

We do not have to choose between loving God or loving our country. God is first, of course, but we can do both. Our country is a Christian nation based on Christian principles, so how could we not love our country? How could we not love our fellow citizens enough to fight to make this country better for everyone?

Our government was created to protect our rights, and part of our rights are our Christian rights. If we don't stand up to protect them, who will?

The answer is, *no one.* Because we've seen what happens when Christians do not engage in government: They forfeit their rights and eventually their freedom. Is there such a thing as being overly patriotic? Not as long as you operate in love and according to God's Word.

Do you know what is lethal, deadly and fatal to Marxism, humanism, secularism, socialism and communism? The answer is patriotism! Do you know what is lethal, deadly and fatal to patriotism? Historical ignorance! Historical amnesia is a free pass for all the "isms" to operate without resistance!

Once patriotism (our Christian civic responsibility) was no longer proclaimed from the pulpits of most of our churches in our nation, the door of socialism was flung wide open and these beliefs are now rooted in the hearts of many of our citizens. In a Christian nation where patriotism is separated from Christianity, the life of liberty is systematically destroyed.

When it comes to standing up for your home, your neighborhood, your community, and your country, it's really a matter of stewardship. It is essential to become an educated voter and get involved in government, because the United States is a "we the people" government.

POLITICS OR PATRIOTISM?

As I said in Chapter 1, this is not a political book. I don't write and teach about politics—I share about our history of Godly principles in action, and how they produce blessings for citizens.

Politics can be an ugly word because our Founders did not set up "politicians," they set up stewards who were public servants. Over time, we elected professional politicians instead of public servants and the negative consequences are evident in our country today.

This Christian nation was established on Godly principles. We are the nation that has propagated the Gospel to the entire world, like no other nation has ever done.

Even though we are a republic, like some other nations, our government is unique in that it was founded on Godly principles by people who wanted to honor biblical concepts. There were some laws and practices that were unjust and needed to be corrected, but until recently the right has far outweighed the wrong. Because of ignorance, the wrong is now beginning to outweigh the right; the moral principles that were once a standard are gradually being abandoned.

Those who believe differently than we do often want Christians to stay in their churches and be quiet. Evil always wants good to stay silent. Evil likes to work in the dark, in sneaky and silent ways, so it can gain ground without recognition. Much of the damage done to our educational system was done secretively, otherwise it might have been exposed and dealt with.

We cannot stay quiet any longer and expect to retain our remaining rights.

THE SUPPORT SYSTEM OF A PATRIOTIC NATION

How can a society survive when its support system has been compromised? What *is* society's support system in a healthy nation?

Following are the three essential parts of a support system—the elements of America's support system when we were a healthier nation:

First, the support system that established America as a society and developed it into a healthy nation all began with *the family*. When a baby (a member of society) is born into a healthy family where it is welcomed, loved, cherished, nourished, cared for and properly taught, it is on its way to becoming a part of a healthy society.

The second element that produced a healthy nation was a *healthy church*. This is where a child grows and matures through the knowledge of God's Word and the guidance of the Holy Spirit. In this atmosphere, a child learns to apply God's principles to his or her decisions and becomes a strong addition to a healthy society.

Third, a healthy society was built upon a *healthy educational system*. It is here where the same principles learned in a healthy home and church are taught and applied in academia. This guarantees that a young person has a solid spiritual and secular foundation that will establish and solidify a healthy society.

These are the three systems that form a healthy society. It was this formative foundation that created our patriotic nation—a patriotism that was revealed in the attitude of the people's appreciation for and mentality to protect what we inherited.

When one or all of these systems fail to function in the format described above, patriotism is paralyzed and society begins to malfunction. Without correction, it eventually becomes dysfunctional.

Through ignorance of who we once were, America's support system is being dismantled. Our patriotism is deteriorating as our nation is being programmed into taking this unhealthy and dysfunctional path. If we as individuals and a nation are to become healthy again, we must restore our support systems.

Our true history tells us who we were, shows us *how we became* who we were, and teaches us what needs to be done to again become the healthy nation we once were.

The question is this: Will we as a nation learn our true history, which teaches us this format, and then be willing to invest the time and energy needed to apply this format?

Time will tell!

WHAT IT MEANS TO BE A PATRIOT

On July 4, 1776, representatives of the Second Continental Congress gathered to sign one of the most important and ambitious documents in history—*the Declaration of Independence.* That day, at the Pennsylvania State House, our Founders didn't know if they were signing their death warrant or the birth certificate of a brand-new nation.

They put everything on the line, and nothing was for certain. If America lost the Revolutionary War, they knew it likely meant death for themselves and even their families. The final line of the Declaration of Independence is filled with their resolve. It proclaims: "With a firm reliance on the protection of Divine Providence, we mutually pledge to each other our lives, our fortunes and our sacred honor."[2]

The colonists came out of an oppressive monarchy in England, and they knew they couldn't go back. In fact, they were willing to pay the ultimate price for their freedom.

The patriotism of our Founding Fathers required tremendous courage for them to be responsible and step out into what God had called them to do. And today, we are still reaping the dividends of their courage. My definition of *courage* is "a willingness and ability to risk who you are and what you have for what you want and who you want to be."

It's important to note that courage cannot function in an atmosphere of ignorance—it has no ability. Courage is the highest expression of responsibility, and responsibility requires knowledge. It requires courage to follow God's plan for our lives and take steps of faith. So often, in order to move forward and have everything He wants us to have, we have to be willing to step out of our comfort zone and take a risk.

In modern times, when it comes to America, people are not often willing to risk much for their country because they don't realize that everything we have was costly. *It wasn't free.* To *gain* freedom is not free, and to *maintain* it is not free.

Yes, patriotism includes celebrating our country on Independence Day and supporting our troops and honoring them on Memorial Day and Veterans Day. *But it is so much more.*

I love the definition of patriotism in Webster's 1828 Dictionary. It is *the passion which aims to serve one's country in defending it from invasion*—which is what the brave men and women of our armed forces have chosen to do. They have chosen to put themselves in harm's way—to sacrifice life and limb—and many of them have suffered in ways that most of us cannot imagine, often without any recognition. They have made this amazing sacrifice of living in harm's way so that the rest of us— and even other nations—might live in freedom. These brave men and women are true patriots and deserve the honor and recognition of every American. Whenever and wherever you see a member of our armed forces who currently serves or has served in the past, let them know how much you appreciate their sacrifice.

But this is not the end of patriotism. The second half of the definition involves every American. It is this: *the passion which aims to serve one's country in protecting its rights and maintaining its laws and institutions of vigor and purity. Patriotism is the characteristic of a good citizen. It's the noblest passion that animates* [makes a man or woman come alive] *in the character of a citizen.*

Our institutions of vigor are our military, our police force, our firefighters, and other first responders. Each of these are vital to our blessed way of life and should be highly respected, honored and appreciated. Our institutions of purity are our families, churches and schools. Each of these—until the last 60 years—had been instrumental in preparing us for our Christian civic responsibilities. This is the part that concerns me: We as individuals and as a nation have not been fulfilling our patriotic civic responsibilities and, as a result, our moral foundation is deteriorating. But this can change if we all join together in fulfilling our patriotic and Christian responsibilities.

Over 240 years ago, standing in what is now called Independence Hall, our Founders literally risked everything for our freedom. And now it's our turn to fight the good fight.

One of my favorite statements was uttered by John Hancock after he signed the Declaration of Independence. He said, "And having secured the approbation [approval] of our hearts by a faithful and unwearied discharge of our duty to our country, let us joyfully leave our concerns in the hands of Him who raiseth up and pulleth down the empires and kingdoms of the world as He pleases."

It's part of our responsibility as citizens. *It's what it means to be a patriot.*

A SOLDIER'S QUESTION

When a soldier returns to civilian life and sees the flag that represents the freedom they fought to preserve being burned, they ask, "*Why?*"

When they see this flag, which many of their friends sacrificed their lives or limbs for, being disrespected, they ask, "*Why?*"

When they notice that some people will not show the courage to just stand and honor the flag while our national anthem is being played, they again ask, "*Why?*"

When they see violent riots in the streets of major cities and police cars and businesses burning, while at the same time the response of police officers is restricted by elected government officials, they ask, "*Why?*"

When entire police departments are defunded because of the unlawful acts of a few, they ask, "*Why?*"

I had the privilege of serving in the United States military. Why did I do what I did? Because I was raised to love my country and believe it was an honor to serve my nation and protect the freedom I cherish—freedom that I could experience because others before me had sacrificed. I was raised to be a patriot.

In those days, there was such a patriotism and respect for those who served. When I returned home after my service, I can vividly remember standing on the deck of our ship as we sailed past the Statue of Liberty. It was such an honor, and I got emotional because it represented the country I loved and would have died to protect.

You see, for several years, I had been serving in other countries, and I experienced the stark contrast between these nations and the United States. During this time, I came to have even more respect for the freedoms and principles we held in America. So, as we sailed by the Statue of Liberty, it represented something extremely special. I was so proud of my country—a country that I loved and served; a country that was welcoming me home with open arms of appreciation.

Today, it's a different story. To many, if not most people, the Statue of Liberty no longer represents what it meant to me that day when I sailed into New York Harbor. So many are unaware of the precious treasures we have been given. As a result, many of those who enter the service today with a passionate and patriotic attitude often return home feeling sorry for the sacrifices they have made to protect the freedom of what has become an uncaring, unpatriotic country.

Since those days when I served from 1960-1963, when patriotism was still healthy, I have seen what has happened to my country, and I'm ashamed of what it has become. It makes me sad when I think of these young men and women, who had such a giant heart to serve their country, often returning to a thankless and unappreciative people.

Even most of the churches of our nation have failed to see the opportunity to welcome them with open arms. If they would have, these confused and broken men and women would have flooded into the kingdom of God, where they could have been shown appreciation and loved back to health.

Instead, they were left on their own to try and make sense out of a senseless situation. As a result of being abandoned, many of them took their own lives since they had no support system to help them adjust.

Tragically, many of the courageous, patriotic, freedom-loving, freedom-protecting young men and women of our country have been lost. So, you tell me, who is left to fight for our freedom? The sad thing is, many in our country don't know or don't care.

That, my friends, is the sad story of the condition of our country since God has been removed from our government, our schools and our history. It is quite a change from the joyous conditions that existed when God was welcome in our government and schools and

His presence was revealed throughout our history.

For all of us in America who still love our country and still have a spark of patriotism left in our hearts, there is a question we need to answer. The question is: *What are we going to do about it?* Are we going to passively turn our heads as that spark fades...or will we allow that spark to once again become a raging fire of patriotism?

Here are four stories from our friends at Alliance Defending Freedom that show how we can put our faith into positive action.

RELATIVISM OR TRUTH?
(Contribution from Alliance Defending Freedom)

Remember not too long ago, when academia and other societal elites told us there were no moral absolutes? Every person could decide for themselves what is right and what is wrong.

There were even entire school courses built around this premise. One popular program was called "Values Clarification." Academics challenged the idea that education should center on the pursuit of truth. After all, truth was relative to the individual.

Francis Schaeffer, one of the best Christian thinkers of the last century, spoke in 1981 at Notre Dame Law School and said that pluralism was always a

temporary state marking a transition from one orthodoxy to another. The advocates of relativism wrapped
themselves in the mantle of pluralism—back in the day.

But now the pretense is over. The new orthodoxy has
arrived, and it intends to purge society of all contrary
views. Social media giants and their fact-checkers are
just the tip of the progressive orthodoxy power structure, which is on the hunt for dissenters who deviate
from its official views.

The cancel culture that seeks to de-platform, destroy
and silence anyone who disagrees with the new orthodoxy manifests itself in a wide array of venues, from
the boardrooms of mega-corporations to the historic
monuments of public parks.

The new orthodoxy has a checklist of its tenets that
cover sexuality, environment, economics and more. But
one thing it does not believe in is freedom—especially
freedom of speech and freedom of religion.

So, what is the Christian response? Two things.

First, during the "truth is relative" era, many Christians were cowed into silence under the theory that
we should not "force" our views on others. That was
an error then, and it is a far more obvious error today.

Citizens should speak and live consistently with
their beliefs and not shy away from it because of social
pressure. Backing down is the path to surrender. I'm
not talking about getting up and shaking your fist or

trying to force your views on others. I'm talking about simply declining to hide the way you have always lived: as a Christian. These are the times when it is especially important to keep speaking and believing according to your faith—more important than when your values are not under threat.

And every citizen should vote based on their values. This means Christians should vote based on their beliefs. It's your right—one that many people around the world would give anything for—and it's a civic duty you should consider an honor to exercise.

Second, Christians should remember that freedom is a biblical value—one that means we stand for freedom for all faiths and all viewpoints. Even when we think those who don't share our values are clearly wrong, it is our duty to stand up for their freedom of speech and religion.

Part of the reason many Christians were confused in the recent era of relativism was because there was a failure to understand the true definition of freedom. Freedom does not teach that all viewpoints are equally valid. Freedom teaches that all viewpoints have the equal right to be freely and peacefully expressed.

Christianity provides a basis for this kind of an approach to freedom. We believe that the mind, heart and soul are the province of God and the individual, not the government.

Freedom for all is a core value of our faith and our nation. Let's vigorously defend it lest we lose that for ourselves and our neighbors.

NO MATTER THE COST
(Contribution from Michael Farris, President and CEO of Alliance Defending Freedom)

Christian viewpoints have rarely been truly popular in my lifetime—at least among many elites in the media, Hollywood, academia, and in certain sectors of political life. These forces have often disagreed with Christian views, but now disagreement has turned to demonizing. There is no more room for agreeing to disagree. People of faith who fail to ratify the dogma of elites will be vilified and worse.

If you believe that marriage is the union of one man and one woman, they accuse you of having hostility toward people who don't share that view. If you believe that human beings are created male and female, they claim that you despise people who identify differently. If you believe that life begins at conception, then you hate women—or so our accusers contend.

That faithful Christians are hated for their beliefs should come as no surprise. Jesus Himself says that *...you will be hated by all for My name's sake...* (Matthew 10:22 NKJV).

This kind of opposition was on full display at a rally that took place on the day of oral arguments in the Harris Funeral Homes court case. As a group gathered to show its support for the view that "sex" should not be redefined to include "gender identity," activists taunted supporters and cursed at children. One woman used a bullhorn to scream insults—for two hours.

The tactics used by these activists are uncivil at best. But the call to all faithful Christians is to stay true to their beliefs despite cultural—and sometimes governmental—pressure. In Luke 14:28, Jesus instructs us to "count the cost" of following Him.

Standing will mean enduring ridicule. It may mean losing your job. It might even mean losing friends or being ostracized by your family. I fear that the repercussions may escalate even beyond all this.

In the end, we all must count which cost is greater: following Christ, or forsaking Him?

STANDING UP FOR OUR RIGHTS
(Contribution from Michael Farris, President and CEO of Alliance Defending Freedom)

Brian Hickman loved to sing and perform to Christian music—something he had learned to do at church. So when his elementary school announced auditions for an upcoming talent show, Brian saw the perfect opportunity to showcase his love for performing. He chose to perform movements to the song "We Shine."

But after auditioning for the talent show, the school principal called Brian's mother to explain that Brian had to pick a different song. The principal claimed the song said "Jesus" too many times and that it would be offensive to people.

Yet the school found nothing objectionable in other songs that were approved for the elementary school show, including songs that discussed teenage "love" and relationship problems, or ones that included suggestive dancing or violent imagery. With the talent show just days away, Brian's family called Alliance Defending Freedom for help.

Brian filed a lawsuit against the Los Angeles Unified School District—one of the largest in the country—challenging the censorship of his talent. Within days, the school reversed course and announced that Brian would be permitted to perform his religious song.

RIGHT TO FREE SPEECH
(Contribution from Michael Farris, President and CEO of Alliance Defending Freedom)

In 2016, Chike was prevented from exercising his right to free speech when officials repeatedly stopped him from peacefully sharing the Gospel with his peers at the college. Since then, with the help of Alliance Defending Freedom (ADF), Chike filed a lawsuit. And while his legal stand has already made a difference for the students that have come after him, courts have continued to deny Chike justice.

The U.S. Supreme Court announced that it would hear Chike's case and give him another chance to get the justice he deserves.

Chike's journey to the Supreme Court started in July 2016 when he was handing out pamphlets in a plaza on campus and talking about the Gospel with interested students as they passed. College officials quickly approached him and ordered him to stop. They informed Chike that if he wanted to distribute materials or talk to his peers about his beliefs, he had to reserve time in the campus "speech zone."

While many public colleges and universities like to advertise speech zones as a place where students can go to speak freely, these types of policies actually restrict free speech. And that's exactly what they did at Georgia Gwinnett College.

Combined, the college's two tiny speech zones made up about 0.0015 percent of campus. In other words, if the entire campus was the size of a football field, these zones—the only places students could exercise their First Amendment rights—would be the size of a piece of paper. On top of that, they were only open to students for a total of 18 hours during the week and were closed on the weekend—which amounts to about 10 percent of the week.

That's not much space or time for free speech, something colleges should cherish and protect at all times and in all generally accessible outdoor areas of campus.

Undeterred, Chike reserved a speech zone and got approval to speak there. But when he began sharing his faith in the speech zone during his reserved time, officials again told him to stop. This time, campus police said it was because someone had complained. Under the *Student Code of Conduct*, any speech "which disturbs the peace and/or comfort of person(s)" qualifies as "disorderly conduct." And that's how officials treated Chike's peaceful speech.

That's why ADF filed a lawsuit on Chike's behalf.

Despite the clear constitutional violations, the college initially did not back down. In its first motion to dismiss the case, the college said that Chike's sharing of the Gospel "arguably rose to the level of 'fighting words,'" a category of speech the First Amendment does not protect.

Eventually, the college abandoned this argument and amended its policies to allow for speech in any outdoor area of campus, likely an effort to evade accountability in the lawsuit. Because of this and the fact that Chike graduated, a federal district court dismissed the case, and the U.S. Court of Appeals for the 11th Circuit upheld that ruling.

But the fact remains that college officials violated Chike's right to free speech—twice. Yet they did nothing to compensate him for this. The government should not be able to violate someone's rights and then walk away as if nothing at all had happened.

That's why Chike asked the U.S. Supreme Court to hear his case.

The Supreme Court needs to make it clear that colleges cannot violate a student's rights, then simply amend their unconstitutional policies after getting sued to avoid the consequences.

These policies hurt real people. People like Chike. And we are grateful that the U.S. Supreme Court is willing to give him another chance at obtaining justice.

PATRIOTISM 101

In today's ever-changing world, it's easy to become negative and want to detach ourselves from our Christian civic responsibilities. There's a prevailing defeated attitude—even among Christians—that says, "What can I do? Can I really make a difference? Does my vote even matter?"

It's this mindset that causes us to be passive

observers instead of active participators. However, the Lord has made each of us stewards of this nation—and this includes our rights and opportunities as citizens of the United States. In short, we have a responsibility to take action and promote biblical principles in any way we can.

The people in many nations do not have a voice in their government—they live in fear, without the freedom to speak freely or worship as they choose. It's time for us to take responsibility and protect what has been given to us. Voting is a privilege that should not be taken for granted. Regardless of how things may seem, *our votes can and do make a difference.*

It's easy to underestimate the value of our vote. Throughout history, many elections were won or lost by only one vote.

- California, Idaho, Oregon, Texas and Washington became states by just ONE vote.
- In 1948, Lyndon B. Johnson, our 36th president, became a U.S. senator by just ONE vote.
- The Declaration of Independence required a majority vote to be accepted and it did so by just ONE vote.[3]

Each and every vote represents the voice of a citizen of the United States of America. One vote speaking out can literally change the course of history. Sadly, only about 50 percent of Christians in America are registered to vote. Then, only half of those 50 percent actually show up at the polls. That means 75 percent of all Christians are not taking advantage of one of their greatest opportunities to shape and protect this nation.[4]

I believe when we take responsibility and do what we can do, then God will do what we can't do. We cannot do God's part, and He will not do our part.

I love Proverbs 29:2, which says, *When the [uncompromisingly] righteous are in authority, the people rejoice; but when the wicked man rules, the people groan and sigh.*

In order to maintain this nation we cherish, it is vital for us to vote based on our beliefs and values—and vote for leaders who stand up for righteousness.

You've probably figured out that watching the political commercials on TV isn't going to give you all of the information you need to make an educated decision. In fact, it may confuse you even more!

I encourage you to visit **joycemeyer.org/america** to find a voter's guide and helpful information.

Much more is at stake than most Christians know. God is watching to see if His people will fulfill their responsibilities and protect the freedom He has blessed them with. If you're not registered to vote, I encourage you to take a few moments to register today.

A CHRISTIAN AND A PATRIOT?

In a Christian nation, Christianity does not govern, but it should govern those who govern!

Now it's your turn to decide. Will you be a Christian *and* a patriot?

CHAPTER 10

Revival or Restoration?

"Not until I went into the churches of
America and heard her pulpits aflame with
righteousness did I understand the secret
of her genius and power."
—attributed to Alexis de Tocqueville,
French political scientist and historian

"If our politics become so corrupt that the very
foundations of our government are ready to
fall away, the pulpit is responsible for it."
—Charles Finney

When it comes to praying for our nation and society,
we often pray for revival when we're actually crying
out for restoration.

When a person's heart fails and a defibrillator is
used to bring the person back to life, they have been

revived. After they have been brought back from the brink of death, they can begin to take steps to improve their diet, add some exercise, and take better care of themselves in order to *restore* their health. Revival and restoration are related, and we need both.

Revival is movement *toward* restoration. In America, both are fueled by knowledge of our history and understanding of how our civil society operates.

Through accurate knowledge of our history, we gain the understanding of how we have been held prisoners in this state of passivity. We also acquire knowledge to fulfill our Christian civic responsibilities and take back the rights and authority that have been stolen. This knowledge of our past—and the resulting actions—will be our revival, and it will lead to our eventual restoration.

Revival without restorative action is not revival at all—it's merely emotion. For example, prayer meetings and rallies can be effective, but if no measurable restoration is achieved after the gathering, the fruitfulness of these experiences is in question.

We have become event oriented instead of responsibility oriented. Responsibility is not an act that is mimicked, but it's an action that stems from knowledge. A few right events will not fix a lifetime of unfulfilled responsibility.

History gives us information on exactly how to gain

back what was lost and protect our future. In the Old Testament, God told the Israelites to remember all the great and mighty things He did for them. But over and over, they forgot and went backward. God was looking for obedience. Obedience only comes through accurate knowledge.

Restoration, as implied in the Word of God, is the knowledge of what was deemed good by God, and then the obedience to re-establish that goodness in our individual lives and our country.

For Israel, this meant restoring their knowledge of God to recreate their relationship with Him, and in doing so, receive their blessings from Him. For us today, this means restoring what God has given us in this country through our Founders: a government founded on Godly principles.

There are many ways restoration can be expressed. For instance, the work our ministry does at the *St. Louis Dream Center* is an example of restoration. The *Dream Center* is an outreach of *Joyce Meyer Ministries* focused on sharing Christ and bringing practical and spiritual help to the St. Louis inner city. Not only are we restoring lives, but by the grace of God, we've made an impact on the neighborhood. Work like this is essential, as well as taking action to restore our society on a *national* level. Our nation's restoration comes through gaining knowledge and taking action to fulfill our Christian civil and moral responsibilities.

RESTORING OUR RIGHTS

A prime biblical example of restoration is recorded in the book of Nehemiah. The people of Israel were well aware that a protective wall used to be there. But unless the Israelites were willing to get their hands dirty, so to speak, and pick up some rocks or grab a shovel, the restoration would not have happened. Notice that the effort took a committed mind and heart.

*So, we built the wall, and all [of it] was joined together to half its height, for the people had a **heart and mind to work*** (Nehemiah 4:6, emphasis added).

We, as individuals and a nation, can be spiritually knowledgeable yet historically ignorant. As a result, we can suffer personally, practically and politically.

Personally, we will lose our identity. We don't know who we are, what our responsibilities are, or what our past consists of.

Practically, we will lose our rights. We have little or no idea of what they are and consequently have no ability to protect them.

Politically, we will either not vote, or we will vote destructively. Voting for whoever makes the biggest promises, without checking their past record (which reveals their character) is destructive to our society.

Why would we vote for such people? Because of historical ignorance we are desensitized and therefore passive, powerless and hopeless. But correct historical knowledge gives us direction for required action.

The following passage is attributed to Alexis de Tocqueville, a French political scientist and historian who visited the United States in the early 1800s:

> "I sought for the greatness and genius of America in her commodious harbors and her ample rivers—and it was not there...in her fertile fields and boundless forests—and it was not there...in her rich mines and her vast world commerce—and it was not there...in her democratic Congress and her matchless Constitution—and it was not there. Not until I went into the churches of America and heard her pulpits aflame with righteousness did I understand the secret of her genius and power. America is great because she is good, and if America ever ceases to be good, she will cease to be great."[1]

Rev. Charles Finney, a minister and leader in America's Second Great Awakening, said:

> "Brethren, our preaching will bear its legitimate fruits.
> If immorality prevails in the land,
> the fault is ours in a great degree.

If there is a decay of conscience,
the pulpit is responsible for it.
If the public press lacks moral discrimination,
the pulpit is responsible for it.
If the church is degenerate and worldly,
the pulpit is responsible for it.
If the world loses its interest in religion,
the pulpit is responsible for it.
If Satan rules in our halls of legislation,
the pulpit is responsible for it.
If our politics become so corrupt that the very foundations of our government are ready to fall away,
the pulpit is responsible for it.
Let us not ignore this fact, my dear brethren; but let
us lay it to heart, and be thoroughly awake to our
responsibility in respect to the morals of this nation."[2]

Responsibility is premeditated accountability that
yields present and future blessings. However, when we
do not take responsibility for what we are responsible
for, we are made responsible for our irresponsibility. It's
called accountability! Accountability, resulting from
failed responsibility, yields present and future penalties.

God will not vindicate those who are irresponsible
due to ignorance. Nor can we hide our incompetence
behind our religiosity and think we are unaccountable.

America is presently being held accountable for

not being responsible for what God has given her. The Church, throughout our history, has been the conscience of our nation and has fulfilled its God-ordained responsibilities. As the conscience of America, the Church has a major role in teaching our Christian civic responsibilities to others in order to protect our constitutional rights. These rights protect the freedoms we enjoy, including the freedom of religion—the right to worship freely.

The Church is mighty and powerful, but only if right action is taken. Ministers must be committed to teaching our Christian civic responsibilities, as was done the first 300 years of our nation's history. How else will Christians know their responsibilities, since they are no longer taught in our schools, in many of our homes, or in the media.

In the last 60 years, the Church has withdrawn from its responsibilities and the consequences have been devastating.

Proverbs 29:18 says, *Where there is no vision [no redemptive revelation of God], the people perish; but he who keeps the law [of God, which includes that of man]—blessed (happy, fortunate, and enviable) is he.*

In this verse, "the people" refers to the unsaved—those who do not have a relationship with God.

So, when the redemptive revelation of God is no longer evident in the responsible, uncompromising daily life of the Body of Christ—when they no longer fulfill their Christian civic responsibilities and stand up for the rights of the people as they did for a century and a half—the people perish. The people no longer see the Church as a relevant example that gives them direction for responsible action. Because the Church— their example—has lost its vision (and therefore its effectiveness), the people have become discouraged, helpless and hopeless, which creates an open invitation for them to be programmed into socialism.

A complacent Church and a Christian nation cannot coexist; both will eventually die!

Moral failure occurs when moral people fail to maintain the moral standard. This is usually due to silence, because of ignorance, which results in irresponsibility. Not doing what needs to be done in the face of evil encourages its growth. Evil is denied existence by wise action, but it abounds because of silence or indifference. Ignorant silence is a result of people not knowing what to do. Indifference is knowing what to do and choosing to do nothing.

THE PROCESS OF THE ELIMINATION OF JUSTICE

When the First Amendment of the Constitution was misinterpreted by an unelected official with very little opposition from the Church, a transfer of power took place.

Since the day the United States was birthed as a constitutional republic (a government of the people, by the people and for the people), the power, authority and responsibility were placed in the hands of the people. This power, authority and responsibility could not be removed from the people unless it was yielded *by the people* through a lack of responsible maintenance.

This is what happened in 1947 when the First Amendment was misinterpreted. The Church did not apply its rightful authority—it didn't fulfill its responsibility to deny the unconstitutional ruling of the separation of church and state. As a result, the constitutional rights of the Church were violated and a portion of the Church's authority was relinquished, never to be recovered.

This abuse of power was enacted by an unelected official of the Supreme Court. And the abuse was committed without the proper responsible action from the people. It was the first major step in removing the *power* from the people and dismantling the *courage* of the people.

By the removal of the Church (the conscience of the country) from government by the misinterpretation of the First Amendment, the Supreme Court had successfully eliminated God's interference in any ungodly government decisions.

By not courageously responding at a critical time in

history, the Body of Christ—the conscience and heart of our nation—was silenced and has never recovered its courage and voice.

Which is more important: Authority or the enforcement of authority? When authority is not applied in situations when it is required, its value and power are eliminated! Justice can no longer be served because its platform has been weakened.

The second major step to remove the authority and power of the people took place in 1962 and 1963 when prayer, the Bible and the Ten Commandments were removed from public schools. This ruling took place to test the will of the people to see if they would passively accept or courageously challenge this violation of their rights.

By 1962, the heart and voice of the Body of Christ had already been silenced by the acceptance of the separation of church and state. As a result, Christian resistance was no longer an issue—the once strong will of the people and consequent responsible action had vanished. So, prayer and the Bible were easily removed, and more of the power and authority once held by the people was confiscated by the government.

This same procedure—to enhance and enlarge government through the removal of the power and authority of the people—has happened over and over again. And all along the way, our history has been revised and God has slowly been erased.

It wasn't long before our educational system was hijacked by humanists, Marxists and socialists, while the citizens of our nation were in a historical coma. They were asleep while our youth, the future of our nation, were being programmed into ignorance.

We have now arrived at a state that would have seemed impossible a few decades ago. Today, so many of our lawyers, judges and politicians are being corrupted, and even our once honorable privilege of voting has been polluted with corruption and fraud.

The sad thing is that the condition of America is not a result of those who are corrupt—it's a result of the passive people. Those who are corrupt only occupy their positions because the passive, good people have not fulfilled their responsibility to act.

This is the story of our government—a government that was created by the people to be a servant of the people…and to protect the rights of the people, who were the master.

It is also the story of how the people, who were the master, are becoming the servant to the government, who *was* the servant. The government is now becoming the master through the irresponsible negligence of "we the people" who were created to be the master.

Evil is provided free access when good provides no resistance!

Although there are many wonderful, active churches, there are still too many of America's churches that are functionally irrelevant because they are historically ignorant. For the most part, the Church knows little or nothing about its extraordinary American Godly heritage. Therefore, it is untrained, unequipped and unqualified to function as the army of God and fulfill its Christian civic responsibilities. Consequently, we are forfeiting our rights and our authority, and therefore our freedom.

THE IMPORTANCE OF GOD IN GOVERNMENT

In another message, Rev. Charles Finney proclaimed: "The church must take right ground in regard to politics...The time has come that Christians must vote for honest men and take consistent ground in politics... God cannot sustain this free and blessed country which we love and pray for unless the Church will take right ground. Politics are a part of religion in such a country as this, and Christians must do their duty to the country as a part of their duty to God. He [God] will bless or curse this nation according to the course they [Christians] take [in politics]."[3]

Around the same time Rev. Finney was preaching revival, President James A. Garfield said this:

"Now more than ever, the people are responsible for the character of their Congress. If that body be ignorant, reckless, and corrupt, it is because the people tolerate ignorance, recklessness, and corruption. If it be intelligent, brave, and pure, it is because the people demand these high qualities to represent them in the national legislature….If the next centennial does not find us a great nation…it will be because those who represent the enterprise, the culture, and the morality of the nation do not aid in controlling the political forces."[4]

Ken Connor, founder of the Center for a Just Society, made this important statement:

In the final analyses, we, the people, are responsible for the corruption of our leaders by failing to demand a higher standard of conduct from our politicians. Increasingly, Americans have grown accustomed to a culture characterized by moral relativism and individualism. We have mocked Judeo-Christian values—humility, virtue, and honor—and in the process, eroded restraints on social conduct. The results have become painfully obvious in the business arena and are becoming increasingly obvious in the political arena.

When we do not demand honor, virtue, and accountability from ourselves, can we really expect more from our leaders? Have we merely gotten the leaders we deserve? The path for reform in the political arena runs straight through the people. We, the people, must first find a renewed appreciation for virtue, honesty, and humility in ourselves and our fellow man. If private virtue is reestablished in society, it will eventually become public and inevitably find its way back to the halls of government. Quite simply, it is up to us.[5]

In the first paragraph of Mr. Connor's quote, I would add the phrase "been programmed to become" after the word "grown." It would then read: "Increasingly, Americans have grown (*been programmed to become*) accustomed to a culture characterized by moral relativism and individualism." This has been an intentional effort by those who oppose this nation's founding principles.

Toward the end of his statement, Mr. Connor says, "We, the people, must first find a renewed appreciation for virtue, honesty, and humility in ourselves and our fellow man." The question is, *how* do we find this appreciation and enact these Godly principles, since God and His principles have been removed from our schools and history books?

The answer is found in God's Word, where His principles are found and the required application and glorious results are revealed. Our true history reveals how our Founders, and the generations that came after them, applied God's principles in their lives and instilled them in the hearts and minds of their children.

There are two major reasons why America became the greatest nation the world has ever known:

1. Dedication to God's Word. (Knowledge of His Word and application of His principles)
2. Dedication to God's business. (Knowledge of and application of our Christian civic responsibilities)

When a nation is ignorant of who they are, they will go AWOL (Absent Without Official Leave) from their responsibilities.

WE THE PEOPLE

The preamble of the U.S. Constitution says: "We the people of the United States, in order to form a more perfect union, establish justice, insure domestic tranquility, provide for the common defense, promote the general welfare and secure the blessings of liberty to ourselves and our posterity, do ordain and establish this constitution for the United States of America."[6]

Whatever is ordained must be maintained if it is to

be sustained and ultimately retained. Our Constitution is only as strong as the knowledge of it and the action to maintain it by the people who are responsible for it.

The power in our government is divided among three branches—the executive, legislative and judicial branch. Each is separate from the others and has different responsibilities, and each also has checks and balances to protect itself from encroachments by the others. This is referred to as "the separation of powers." When each branch functions in its allotted power and authority as designed by our Founders, the rights of the people are protected and the nation flourishes.

To the degree that any of the branches forfeit their power and authority, to this degree the rights and authority of the people are relinquished. The branches forfeit power and authority because the people do not take responsibility to hold their elected officials accountable; consequently, the elected officials do not take responsibility to act accountably.

The rights and authority of the people directly correlate to the allotted power and authority of the three branches of our government, which can only be held in check by knowledgeable—and therefore responsible—people.

We are a government of the people, by the people and for the people. The failure or success of our government begins and ends with "we the people." We are those people. *I* am one of those people. *You* are one of those people. I cannot fulfill your responsibility for this nation and you cannot fulfill mine. But we can see restoration if we all do our part.

A Christian nation and a complacent Church cannot coexist. Both will eventually die. What happens in a Christian nation with a complacent Church? The people are waiting on God to do what God is waiting on the people to do. They cast their responsibility and complain about their conditions.

We didn't receive our freedom by wishing, and we can't restore it by wishing. But someday we may wish we would have done what was required to keep our freedom.

IS GOD YOUR FIRST RESPONSE OR LAST RESORT?

How does a nation of Christian first responders deteriorate to a nation of Christians who pray as a last resort?

What do Christians do in a Christian nation when its moral foundation is crumbling? They pray for God to restore the morals while many have failed to fulfill their responsibilities to preserve them.

Our moral principles were maintained by patriotic knowledge of our Christian civic responsibilities that once came from the pulpits of our nation. Without moral principles, America's freedom is deteriorating.

Prayer was once our first response, but as a result of a lack of knowledge concerning our patriotic Christian civic responsibilities, prayer has become our last resort.

Throughout our nation's history, prayer included seeking God's guidance and then responding by fulfilling His direction.

Prayer was our first response in times of need. In the last 50 years, prayer has gradually evolved from a position of responding to God in prayer during times of need to praying as a last resort in times of crisis. Most crises take place when responsibility is unfulfilled at the time it is required, resulting in prayer being our last resort.

Prayer as a last resort is asking God to rescue us from our irresponsibility. God may do this if we are repentant and we're willing to learn from our mistakes. But if we continue in irresponsibility after that, we will suffer the consequences. It's called accountability.

America was once a nation of first responders who would recognize any threat to the laws that protect and the rights that guarantee our freedom...and then deal with those threats quickly and decisively.

That's what we as a nation throughout our history were taught to do and always did. This knowledge and ability was passed down from generation to generation through accurate knowledge of our history, and as a result, our freedom was protected and maintained.

In the last century, an evil ideology has arisen in America because our history has been distorted. It has slowly, secretively and methodically changed our nation from being first responders to inactive procrastinators.

If first responders are not properly trained, equipped and qualified to handle the difficult situations they are exposed to, those situations can quickly turn into disasters.

This is what is happening to our once beautiful republic (rule of law) that had been protected by the knowledgeable, and therefore responsible, people that went before us. Our republic is being dismantled. It is deteriorating as our Constitution is being marginalized because we the people have been programmed into ignorance concerning our responsibility to maintain it.

We have arrived at a "last resort" mentality of God rescuing us. Our once healthy freedom is flatlining. Like a person whose heart has failed and their only hope is the use of a defibrillator to revive them, we are asking God to revive our freedom since we have failed in our responsibility to maintain its health.

Like a revived person who is then placed on a proper diet to improve their health, we as a Christian nation must learn and fulfill our forgotten responsibilities, if our freedom is to be healthy again.

There are two books that are vital for every Christian. Number one is the Bible. It instills in you a love for God the Father, your Creator; God the Son, your Deliverer, who paid the price for your salvation by sacrificing His life for your sins, so that you might have opportunity to spend eternity with Him; and God the Holy Spirit, who comes to live in you and reveal the presence of God the Father and God the Son, as well as to teach you and guide you into all truth (see John 16:13).

The Bible reveals that these three—God the Father, God the Son and God the Holy Spirit—are one God who loves each of us so much that He was willing to sacrifice His Son. Jesus, His Son, willingly made this sacrifice to provide the way for us to live in eternity with Him.

There is only one requirement for each individual to obtain this eternal life and live in eternity with God. That requirement is the belief in and acceptance of the sacrifice of His Son for our salvation.

God has provided a way for all of mankind to live in eternity with Him, and that is why the devil does not want you to read the Bible.

Number two is our true American history, which teaches how the principles of the Bible were applied in the lives of our Founders and in the founding documents of our nation.

Those Godly men produced documents containing the principles of the Bible, which provided the freedom we have been blessed to experience in America. This is why it is critical for us to know our history, which provides the knowledge needed to protect the health of our freedom.

America was and is a Christian nation, and as long as we followed biblical guidelines for morality, our nation prospered in every way. But due to large numbers of people turning their backs on God and His ways, our nation is now in sharp decline and has reached the crisis stage. Now is the time to take action—to put God first again and fulfill our civic responsibilities as Christians.

Both of these books are on Satan's "restrict-at-all-cost list." He has worked long and hard to keep Christians and non-Christians from gaining the knowledge contained in these two books.

He knows well the danger these books present to his kingdom of darkness. He also knows the unbridled energy and passion they produce in Christians to fulfill God's destiny in their lives and for their country.

That's why he has spent the last century revising our history and removing God from our history books. His fear of the Truth is very real, because truth exposes his deception and reveals his identity as the father of lies (see John 8:44).

If you are a confused and frustrated Christian or non-Christian, it's because the information you've been taught has been false. Jesus said, "*If you abide in My word...you shall know the truth, and the truth shall make you free*" (John 8:31-32 NKJV).

You may ask, "Free to do what?" The answer is free

to live the life God designed for you to live, complete with His joy and peace.

In most cases, this false information has been introduced into society through the immoral, humanistic public school system. It's time for people to understand that they have been programmed into ignorance and they no longer have to stay that way.

The truth in the Bible—God's Word—is God's gift to you to help you be the person God made you and desires for you to be.

Why would God, who created and controls the universe, do this? Simply because He loves you! After all, that's the reason He created you.

God is merciful, and if we will repent and begin doing our Christian civic duty, He will heal our land. The time is short, but it is not too late to begin going in the right direction!

PRAY IT FORWARD

When it comes to praying for our country, 2 Chronicles 7:14 is undoubtedly the most quoted verse in Scripture. The Lord says:

> *If My people, who are called by My name, shall humble themselves, pray, seek, crave, and require of necessity My face and turn from their wicked ways, then will I hear from heaven, forgive their sin, and heal their land.*

I think it's important to really pay attention when the Lord uses the words "if" and "then" in His Word. It signals that God is giving us a part to play, and if we do *our* part, then He will do *His* part. In the above verse, our part includes four specific things to do: humble ourselves, pray, seek the Lord, and turn from wickedness (unfulfilled responsibility). When we do, *then* God will do His part—He will hear from heaven, forgive our sins, and heal our land.

Prayer is extremely important, and I believe part of my calling is to ignite a passion in people to intercede for America. However, prayer is only one of the ingredients needed. Our part also involves true humility, repentance and responsibility.

We can pray for restoration; however, restoration can't come until there is revival. Revival can't come until there is responsibility. Responsibility can't come until there is repentance, and repentance won't come until we *remember* who we once were—our history.

What types of things should we remember?

- How was our government formed?
- What price was paid for our liberty? And who paid it?
- What role did God play in the lives of our Founders?
- What responsibilities did our Founders give us?

- Who has fought to maintain and restore
  God-given freedoms throughout our history?
- How do these pivotal moments benefit us today?
  And what can we learn from their fight?
- By looking at history, we not only see what we
  should do, but we see things that were done
  wrong and should not be repeated. It educates us
  for the future.

It's been over 25 years since a friend first gave me a copy of the book *America's Providential History*. I'll never forget how God used it to open my eyes to all of the great and mighty things He did to establish this nation. I also learned how, in recent generations, a lack of knowledge concerning our history has slowly chipped away at the Godly foundation laid by our Founders. It pierced my heart and provoked me to pray for America like never before. *This is also my prayer for you.*

I encourage you to set aside some time to pray for America. Pray that God would turn the hearts of our people back to Him, and that we would all learn our history and recover our stolen identity. Pray we would once again honor God and look to Him as our one true source of strength, blessings and protection.

As we pray, it's also vitally important to do what God shows us. This means learning our true history, which will teach us how to accurately fulfill our

Christian civic duties, like contacting our elected officials to let our voices be heard. With your help, and with your diligence, we can protect our liberties. But *without* your help and your diligence, our liberties will continue to be lost.

We each have a tremendously important part to play in restoring the United States. And as we are faithful to do what we *can* do, the Lord will be faithful to do what we can't and bring healing to our land.

THE ROAD TO RESTORATION

The road to restoration that I find in the Bible has five guidelines that must be followed—in the appropriate order. Each of these guidelines starts with the letter R.

The first guideline is REMEMBRANCE. When a person or nation that was once going in the right direction is now headed in the *wrong* direction, it is only through remembrance of their past (history) that they can identify how and when they began to go in the wrong direction.

At this point, the second guideline is applied: REPENTANCE. Repentance means to turn around and go in the right direction.

Then the third guideline, RESPONSIBILITY, is reapplied. I say *reapplied* because it's what we as a nation were doing prior to sliding in the wrong direction.

Once we have become responsible again, we will

enact the fourth guideline, which is REVIVAL. Our lives and our nation will be revived because we have become responsible. And it sure feels good to experience freedom—the fruit of our actions. We will be rejoicing, and God will be rejoicing with us, because our obedience has reopened the pathway for His grace.

As a result of our personal revival, and the revival of our nation, the fifth guideline will be fulfilled: RESTORATION. We and our nation will be restored to our rightful heritage.

Remembrance
Repentance
Responsibility
Revival
Restoration

Remembrance leads to repentance, which creates responsibility. This enacts revival and establishes restoration.

The choice is ours. America the beautiful must become America the dutiful, or it will become America the pitiful. We must become responsible or we will be made accountable.

★★★

CHAPTER 11

Be Strong and Courageous

"Courage is rightly esteemed the first of human qualities...because it is the quality which guarantees all others."[1]
—Winston Churchill

Have not I commanded you? Be strong, vigorous, and very courageous. Be not afraid, neither be dismayed, for the Lord your God is with you wherever you go.
—Joshua 1:9

It's my sincere hope that you realize the value of our true history and how society has been intentionally deceived. And I hope you realize the importance of acting upon the truth to bring about restoration. If we don't take action and fulfill our responsibilities, we are in danger of losing our freedom.

We do not have to accept the decline of this country's culture. Decline is not inevitable if we will simply take our rightful place and exercise our civic duties as Christians.

Please hear me. We don't have to be hopeless about our nation. All we have to do is educate ourselves—and our loved ones—and our path will be made clear. We are not without hope! Things can change and our nation can become extraordinary once again.

But stepping forward onto that path will take courage.

AMERICA'S FUTURE BEGINS WITH YOU AND ME

Since the days of the American Revolution, the United States has been regarded as the greatest and most prosperous nation in the world. For more than 200 years, we have enjoyed unprecedented success and ever-increasing opportunity.

However, in recent years, we have witnessed a startling decline in so many aspects of government and society. The current condition of America can leave us wondering, *How did we manage to shift so far from our original foundation?* And maybe more importantly, *What can we do to fix it?*

We can learn an important lesson from the Israelites. Throughout the Old Testament, God commanded Israel to "never forget the things your eyes have seen" and "teach them to your children and your grandchildren" (see Deuteronomy 4:9).

In fact, the Lord instructs them to literally bind His Word on their hands and their foreheads. Why? God tells them, *Lest when you have eaten and are full, and have built goodly houses and live in them...you forget the Lord your God, Who brought you out of the land of Egypt...* (Deuteronomy 8:12,14).

But after they entered the Promised Land, and life got easier, they began to fall away.

When Godly kings ruled Israel, they were blessed and protected from their enemies. However, when an ungodly king ruled, the nation began to go backward, falling away from God's protection and blessings.

I love the story of King Josiah, who became the king of Judah when he was only 8 years old. Prior to his reign, evil kings had ruled for many years, leading the hearts of the people away from the Lord. When Josiah was 26, the high priest discovered the Book of the Law in the basement of the Temple. It contained all of the laws and instructions given by God to the people of Israel. Consider King Josiah's response:

> And when the king heard the words of the Book of the Law, he rent his clothes. ...Then he said, Go, inquire of the Lord for me and for the people and for all Judah... because our fathers have not listened and obeyed the

words of this book, to do according to all that is writ-
ten concerning us (2 Kings 22:11,13).

King Josiah was overwhelmed because he knew God
was the One who made Israel great—and destruction
was certain if they continued to walk away from Him.
This crossroad is exactly where America is today. If we
continue to drift from the Godly principles that made
us great, we will forfeit our future by failing to remember the past.

America has gone from a *strong, Godly* nation—on
a path to right its past wrongs and bring the promise
of life, liberty and the pursuit of happiness to every
citizen—to a *complaining, complacent* society. Since we
should have done what we didn't do, now we can't do
what we want to do, and all we know to do is blame and
complain. A common comment today is, "All I know is,
it's not my fault that our country is in this condition."

My question is, *Then whose fault is it?* We must all
share the responsibility rather than trying to blame it
on someone else.

If we say it's not our fault that we are in this
condition, let's at least admit that it is our fault if
we stay in this condition. The silent majority has
been passive—not active—for too long. Either we
respond or relinquish the freedom and excellent life
God wants us to enjoy.

So, what can we as Christians do to reverse this course? We must remember who we are, where we came from, what role God played in our government and in the lives of our early leaders, and why it's important to be accountable for what God has given us.

When we discover *Who* and *what* made us great, it provides a compass for our future. Yes, we may have a long way to go, but change *is* possible. Because now we know what we need to do, and we can become responsible patriots for our great nation.

THE CURE FOR A NATION AT RISK

Throughout history, mankind has witnessed the rise and fall of more than 20 great civilizations, and every one of them shared the same "symptoms" that eventually led to their decline. One major warning sign is the loss of respect for *tradition*—a major issue that America faces today.

In many schools today, any traces of God have systematically been removed. Many textbooks also attempt to discredit historical figures in order to discredit their message. For instance, they claim that our Founders never spoke about religion and their motives were based on selfishness and greed. However, overwhelming evidence of their faith in God and service to this nation can be found in nearly every founding document.[2]

As time passes and traditions weaken, the foundational principles once considered essential to a nation are seen as old-fashioned and undesirable. Activists then demand change and seek to revise and erase the past.

American history, as it's currently taught, has been revised, yet no one notices. Why? Because educators, government officials and citizens rarely research the original historical documents. We've reached a place where most people simply "take their word for it."

Failure to know our history has led to widespread gullibility, making us vulnerable to those who want to change our culture. So, what is the cure for a nation at risk? The answer is very simple: Learn biblical history and our true national history, then teach it to your family. Teach them about the things we did wrong that we should never do again, and teach them about the things we did right that we should keep doing.

The future is always an extension of our past. If our past is distorted and evidence of God's handiwork has been removed, our direction for the future will disappear and we will wander aimlessly—just as the Israelites did each time they forgot God. The result is always loss of freedom.

However, if we will take the time to discover our past and all the great and mighty things God has done, we will no longer be deceived. It will give us the direction *and* passion to change course and restore all that we have lost.

Ronald Reagan said, "Freedom is never more than one generation away from extinction."[3] This is why you and I must engage in the struggle and let our voices be heard. First, we must register to vote. As citizens in a Christian nation, voting is a great privilege and responsibility. We must vote for people with strong *principles*, not merely *promises*, then hold our representatives accountable to do what they said they would do.

We must determine that we will not allow our heritage of faith and freedom to be dismantled and revised. Speaking up and taking action might feel scary at first, but as the title of Joyce's recent book declares, we can "do it afraid."

Our true history is a record of a nation that has been protected by ordinary men and women who have displayed extraordinary courage. This courage needs to be displayed on the national stage and in local school board meetings; in churches and at state capitals; and online and in conversations with neighbors.

Knowledge is the answer to anything. Why is knowledge so important? Because a lack of knowledge has such a destructive domino effect. All of the deception we experience in our nation causes people to mistrust one another. This creates an attitude of withdrawal, which causes disengagement of our responsibilities and leads to the relinquishment of our rights—and eventually our freedom.

Hosea 4:6 says, *My people are destroyed for lack of knowledge…* (NKJV).

As you begin to step out and take action, remember this principle. We should share truths about the condition of our society with people who are "wide awake," so to speak. We must share truths about the condition of our society with people who are ready to hear—and pray for those who need a change of heart. We can't talk a passive nation into action. First, people need to wake up to the alarming realities in our nation.

Signs of someone being "asleep" include expressions like, "God will take care of this somehow," "America always rebounds and regains its sanity," and "We're in the end times, so this decline is to be expected."

Share strong facts and historical truths to awaken people. This will spur people to learn *and* take action. If we don't speak boldly and strongly, our message will not impact people.

This is especially important when it comes to educating our children and grandchildren. The reason young people are often overwhelmed and intimidated by worldly culture is because they have no idea what they will encounter when they begin attending school. Unless they are educated and grounded in the truth, they can be swayed.

Here's another story from our friends at Alliance Defending Freedom which shows how we must stand up to protect our freedoms.

PROTECTING CHILDREN AND FAMILIES
(Contribution from Michael Farris, President and CEO of Alliance Defending Freedom)

I was a very young lawyer when I got the call one Monday morning. Child Protective Services (CPS) had seized a couple's son on the previous Friday night. Island County (Washington State) Court would hold a hearing the following day.

The court had given no advance notice. It was an emergency seizure, they believed. Courts reserve such ad hoc removals for the most serious situations, where the child is in such imminent danger that there is no time for a regular hearing.

The allegations were breathtaking—but not in the sense that the parents had done something serious. The charge? The parents took their son to church too much. They went Sunday morning, Sunday evening, and Wednesday night.

It seems that the 13-year-old boy went to his public-school counselor to complain about church. He didn't like it. Again, he was 13.

The counselor called CPS, and it was obvious to

them that an emergency was developing. After all, it was Friday, and Sunday was coming. And on Sunday, he had to go to church twice—surely a clear and present danger to the child!

At the time, Washington State had passed a law that directly parallels the provisions of the United Nations Convention on the Rights of the Child, which has been ratified by every country except the United States. The treaty says that the "best interest of the child" shall control every situation.

Christians need to understand why this standard poses a dangerous threat to the profoundly important parental rights given to us by our Creator.

This innocuous-sounding phrase needs some translation. It is a 400-year-old legal phrase (originally used in family law cases) that once had a good purpose. The "best interest of the child" standard does not seek to determine "what" is best for the child; rather, it determines "who gets to decide."

For hundreds of years under British law and American law, parents decided what is best unless they seriously breached their duties. Normally, the courts had to show that the parent had either abandoned or criminally abused the child before the court could step in.

The Washington law, like the UN treaty, is an effort to strip those basic decision-making rights from parents.

At its root is a progressive view of law that divorces "justice" from absolute truth or historic precedent. This insidious contemporary view states that the best interest of the child shall control in every case. Simply put, the UN treaty and Washington law no longer presume that fit parents are acting in the child's best interest—but instead empower courts to take custody of children when the parents have done no wrong.

Accordingly, the Island County judge got to decide that if my clients wanted to keep custody of their son, they would have to limit his church attendance to once a week. I wanted to appeal. But since I could not guarantee that the parents could keep custody during the appeal, they decided not to do so.

There are too many similar stories, such as a pastor who was threatened with loss of his daughter unless he let her go to the junior prom. Some of the most egregious situations arise in the states that enable children to seek so-called "sex-change" treatments without their parents' permission, or which ban parents from seeking counseling for children struggling with unwanted same-sex attraction.

If your "inner lawyer" is yelling about constitutional rights about now, you have good instincts. Unfortunately, the U.S. Supreme Court's legal reasoning runs contrary to that instinctive sense of what is right. In 2000, the high court decided a case that led to many of these difficulties, and it has yet to correct this wayward decision.

Troxel v. Granville dealt with a grandparent's visitation rights—again in Washington State. Even though the Supreme Court ruled for the parents in the end, only one justice, Clarence Thomas, did so based on traditional, constitutional grounds (the right of parents to direct the upbringing of their child).

This split decision produced a total of six opinions out of nine justices. One justice even wrote that parents have no constitutional rights whatsoever because there is no parental rights amendment in the Constitution.

The attack on parental rights is part of a larger movement to attack God's role in our lives. It is no accident that this movement rides on the back of the near-universal acceptance of evolution. By rejecting God's creation, we eventually reject the family unit that is basic to His created order (see Genesis 2:22–24).

This attitude goes all the way back to the Garden of Eden. After Adam's fall, wickedness and violence spread throughout the earth, requiring God to step in with a universal flood. After the flood, God set up a new social order in Genesis 9, where He expected mankind to intervene (ultimately through governments) to protect human life.

Respect for life has brought blessings to nations

ever since, while violence and abuse of helpless citizens have brought God's judgment (see Amos 1:3–2:3 among many other prophetic passages). Yet government was never intended to replace or supersede the family, which remains the primary institution for raising children.

The Declaration of Independence formalized the United States' aim to honor these basic truths, asserting that we are endowed by our Creator with certain unalienable rights and that governments are instituted to protect those rights.

Every one of us has been a child and many are parents, so this issue impacts literally every living soul. For Christians who understand that God's family-centered created order benefits us all, it is right and proper to make every effort to ensure our government views its highest duty as defending family rights.

After all, the Bible teaches that God raised up governments to be His servants for "good" (see Romans 13:1–4). Those that reject God end up creating fallible "gods" in the form of government officials, who disregard and overturn the family, parenthood, and our roles as men and women.

Defending our God-given liberties begins at home, but it must go further. For those who are directly attacked, it may mean taking a stand in federal court. And all of us can become better informed, educate others, vote for candidates who support biblically consistent laws, and support advocacy groups that further those goals. That way each of us will always "be ready in season and out of season" (2 Timothy 4:2 NKJV) to stand for our civil right and to follow God's design for the family and parents.

BUILD YOUR RELATIONSHIP WITH AMERICA

In so many ways, our lives are built upon relationships. And whether it's our relationship with God, family, friends or even co-workers, every healthy relationship requires our time and attention if we want to see it flourish. It doesn't just happen automatically.

Our relationship with America is no different. The blessings we enjoy today didn't simply happen by accident. They are the result of the prayers, resolve and actions of our predecessors—the ones who forged the way for this nation to succeed.

It is our duty—and privilege—to pick up where they left off. We have to learn what our forefathers did to achieve this incredible freedom and liberty, then do those same things to keep it.

Our Founders said it would take "eternal vigilance" for this country to stay strong. We don't often hear this term anymore, but it simply means we need to maintain *constant responsibility*. It's more than just voting in one crucial election. Eternal vigilance isn't a single event, it's *a way of life.*

I believe most people *want* to do their part and take an active role in this nation. They may even know when something's wrong, but they just don't know how to fix it. And when people don't know what to do, it leads to apathy, passivity, frustration and even deception. The best way to begin building your relationship with America is to take the time to understand our nation's Godly history. I've included some recommended resources in the back of this book.

I promise you, as you educate yourself, it will ignite a passion in your heart to not only pray for America, but also to fulfill your Christian civic responsibilities.

We live in a unique time in history, and it's not an accident—God has prepared each one of us for such a time as this. He is asking us to stand up and take action, not only for ourselves, but also for the sake of future generations.

This is our country, and *together* we can do what it takes to protect the blessings and freedom God has given us.

God is waiting for the Body of Christ in America to become a courageous body. The Lord wants to use our nation, our resources, and our people to once again be a beacon of light, to shine brightly for Jesus Christ all around the world.

Understand the root causes of our decline. Find a

solution you believe in. And take courageous action—motivated by love for God and love for people.

Based on the patriotic statement of Theodore Roosevelt, I will echo his sentiment in my own words: What we know or don't know about our history will determine what we do or don't do with our moment of history, and will make all the difference in our destiny as individuals and as a nation.

AMERICA'S FORMULA TO MAINTAIN FREEDOM

If we will learn our Godly history, we will realize our rights. This will enable us to fulfill our responsibilities and replace professional politicians with faithful stewards whom we will hold accountable to maintain our Constitution. This will protect our freedom to live this blessed life, so we can give God all the glory for allowing us to be a part of His story.

In this book, I have exposed America's problems and revealed the solutions. Now, it's up to each of us to be the answer. I pray God's anointing and blessing on all who will engage in this responsibility.

★★★

ACKNOWLEDGMENTS

Writing this book has been a wonderful experience, and it certainly wouldn't be possible without the help and contributions of several others.

First, I want to thank God for the things He has taught me and for giving me the grace to write this book.

I also want to thank my beautiful and diligent wife, Joyce, whom I love and admire. I appreciate all of your time and help in bringing this project to fruition.

Special thanks also go out to Mike Loomis, who helped me to compile and edit all of the content and information in this book, along with Chad Trafton, who helped edit the manuscript and prepare it for print.

My journey to discovering our nation's true Godly heritage began the day I opened the book *America's Providential History.* So, I'd like to acknowledge the authors, Stephen K. McDowell and Mark A. Beliles. God used your work to ignite a profound passion in my heart for America. The Lord also gave me an unquenchable desire to teach others about His role in establishing this great nation, and how they can take action to preserve the incredible freedoms we have been given.

I also want to thank those who have made significant contributions to this book: Michael Farris and all those at Alliance Defending Freedom; Carole Adams, the president of the Foundation for American Christian Education; and David Barton, one of today's premier scholars, historians, authors and teachers—you have taught me so much, and I continue to learn from all of your wonderful resources.

Finally, I want to recognize a group that is on the front lines of sharing God's plans and purpose for this country—the pastors and Christian leaders who are educating the Body of Christ about their Christian civic responsibilities. In a society where so many seek to censure our Christian heritage and push God away, you are courageously standing up for the One Who truly made this nation great and teaching that God and government have been inextricably joined together. Your actions are making a profound difference, and you are setting the example for other pastors and leaders around the country.

NOTES

INTRODUCTION

1. https://www.dhs.gov/immigration-statistics/ yearbook/2019/table1
2. https://www.nps.gov/stli/learn/historyculture/ colossus.htm

CHAPTER 1

1. https://www.inspiringquotes.us/author/4230-baron-de-montesquieu
2. From John Adams to Massachusetts Militia, October 11, 1798, *Founders Online*, National Archives. www.founders. archives.gov/documents/Adams/99-02-02-3102
3. https://www.quotetab.com/quote/by-karl-marx/ take-away-a-nations-heritage-and-they-are-more-easily-persuaded
4. https://www.azquotes.com/author/20531-Alexander_ Fraser_Tytler
5. https://thefederalistpapers.org/founders/others/john-hancock-speech-commemorating-the-boston-massacre-march-05-1774

CHAPTER 2

1. www.goodreads.com/author/quotes/17142.Edmund_ Burke
2. www.archives.gov/founding-docs/declaration-transcript
3. www.pewresearch.org/fact-tank/2017/02/15/u-s-students-internationally-math-science/
4. www.c250.columbia.edu/c250_celebrates/remarkable_ columbians/john_dewey.html
5. www.brainyquote.com/quotes/vladimir_lenin_153238
6. www.constitution.congress.gov/constitution/ amendment-1/

7. www.goodreads.com/quotes/187182

8. https://www.goodreads.com/quotes/88664-when-the-people-find-that-they-can-vote-themselves-money

9. www.archives.gov/founding-docs/declaration-transcript

10. Ferdon, Gai M., Ph.D. *A Republic If You Can Keep It*, The Foundation for American Christian Education, 2008, p. v.

11. www.archives.gov/founding-docs/declaration-transcript

CHAPTER 3

1. https://www.goodreads.com/quotes/6407-our-lives-begin-to-end-the-day-we-become-silent

2. Maybury, Richard J. *Are You Liberal? Conservative? Or Confused?* Bluestocking Press, Placerville California, 2014, p. 46.

3. *The Founders' Bible*, "Freedom Versus Liberty," Shiloh Road Publishers, 2017, p. 1,860. www.amazon.com/Founders-Bible-David-Barton/dp/161871001X

4. www.americanrhetoric.com/speeches/mlkihaveadream.htm

5. www.constitution.congress.gov/constitution/amendment-1/

6. https://books.google.com/books?id=r9JLAAAAMAAJ&pg=PA307&lpg=PA30

7. Used with permission of The Leadership Institute. www.leadershipinstitute.org

8. www.goodreads.com/quotes/187182

CHAPTER 4

1. https://www.inspiringquotes.us/author/1091-woodrow-wilson

2. https://www.thefreelibrary.com/Reflections+on+reading-a0305838502

3. *American Dictionary of the English Language*, Foundation for American Christian Education, 1967 & 1995.

4. Skousen, W. Cleon. *The 5000 Year Leap: A Miracle That Changed the World*, National Center for Constitutional Studies, 2011, p. xvi.

5. Ibid., p. xvii.

6. https://www.reaganlibrary.gov/research/speeches/01051967a

CHAPTER 5

1. https://www.dictionary.com/browse/those-who-cannot-remember-the-past-are-condemned-to-repeat-it

2. www.azquotes.com/quote/1172318

3. *Journals of the Continental Congress*, Washington: Government Printing Office, 1907, Vol. VIII, p. 734, September 11, 1777.

4. Used with permission from www.wallbuilders.com/aitken-bible-congress

5. https://books.google.com/books?id=sRETAAAAYAAJ&pg=RA1-PA337&lpg=RA1-PA337&dq=Alexis+de+Tocqueville

6. www.brainyquote.com/quotes/abraham_lincoln_133687

CHAPTER 6

1. http://libertytree.ca/quotes/Nikita.Khrushchev.Quote.7174

2. https://www.goodreads.com/work/quotes/4024969-kritik-des-gothaer-programms

3. https://news.gallup.com/poll/257639/four-americans-embrace-form-socialism.aspx

4. http://libertytree.ca/quotes/Josef.Stalin.Quote.CC49

5. http://libertytree.ca/quotes/J..Edgar.Hoover.Quote.5956

6. http://libertytree.ca/quotes/Norman.Thomas.Quote.FFB1

7. http://libertytree.ca/quotes/Ayn.Rand.Quote.E3A6

CHAPTER 7

1. https://books.google.com/books?id=Pd89AAAAIAAJ&pg

2. www.constitution.congress.gov/constitution/amendment-1/

3. Barton, David. *Original Intent*, WallBuilder Press, Aledo, Texas, 2008, pp. 51-52.

4. Sewell, Carol. *What Were They Thinking? On Truth, Liberty & Legacy*, G2g Publishers, Inc., 2009, p. 154.

5. Barton, David. *Original Intent*, WallBuilder Press, Aledo, Texas, 2008, p. 248.

6. Ibid., p. 249.

7. Ibid., p. 252.

8. Ibid., p. 236.

9. Ibid., p. 237.

10. https://founders.archives.gov/documents/Jefferson/01-39-02-0070

11. Hill, Steven. *Fixing Elections: The Failure of America's Winner-Take-All Politics*, Center for Voting and Democracy. https://books.google.com/books/about/Fixing_Elections.html?id=QJKD0pb2OlsC

12. Stein, Joel. "Who's in Charge Here?" *Time*, May 13, 2013, p. 58.

13. www.goodreads.com/quotes/430081

CHAPTER 8

1. https://www.ushistory.org/paine/commonsense/sense5.htm

2. Beliles, Mark A., and McDowell, Stephen K. *America's Providential History*, The Providence Foundation, 1989, pp. 98-99.
3. https://www.azquotes.com/quote/610451 and https://www.azquotes.com/quote/555536
4. Beliles, Mark A., and McDowell, Stephen K. America's Providential History, The Providence Foundation, 1989, pp. 102-103.
5. Ibid., p. 109.

CHAPTER 9

1. *American Dictionary of the English Language*, Foundation for American Christian Education, 1967 & 1995.
2. Barton, David. *Original Intent*, WallBuilder Press, Aledo, Texas, 2008, p. 360.
3. Sewell, Carol. *What Were They Thinking? On Truth, Liberty & Legacy*, G2g Publishers, Inc., 2009, p. 3.
4. https://www.myfaithvotes.org/articles/a-letter-to-pastors-on-a-biblical-requirement-to-vote

CHAPTER 10

1. https://faithandamericanhistory.wordpress.com/2016/07/27/america-is-great-because-america-is-good-part-one/
2. https://preachersinstitute.com/2012/09/18/the-pulpit-is-responsible/
3. Barton, David. *Original Intent*, WallBuilder Press, Aledo, Texas, 2008, p. 354.
4. https://www.azquotes.com/quote/606290

5. Sewell, Carol. *What Were They Thinking? On Truth, Liberty & Legacy*, G2g Publishers, Inc., 2009, p. 18.

6. https://constitution.congress.gov/constitution/preamble

CHAPTER 11

1. https://www.goodreads.com/quotes/121685

2. Barton, David. *Original Intent*, WallBuilder Press, Aledo, Texas, 2008, pp. 293-294.

3. www.reaganlibrary.gov

RECOMMENDED RESOURCES

To help you get started in your search to understand our nation's true history, I've gathered some helpful articles, along with some of the greatest resources I have found on our country's Christian heritage, and have made them available at **joycemeyer.org/america**

Here, you can also find a list of your elected officials and how to contact them, critical information about special issues, and much more. I personally invite you to take some time and visit our site today: **joycemeyer.org/america**

On the following pages are some organizations and books I recommend.

Be blessed!

Dave Meyer

ORGANIZATIONS

Alliance Defending Freedom, ADFLegal.org

Family Research Council, FRC.org

Foundation for American Christian Education
Dr. Carole Adams, FACE.net

Judicial Action Group, JudicialActionGroup.com

The Leadership Institute, LeadershipInstitute.org

National Council on Bible Curriculum in Public Schools
BibleInSchools.net

Vision America, VisionAmerica.org

WallBuilders, Wallbuilders.com

BOOKS

America's Providential History
by Mark A. Beliles and Stephen K. McDowell

The Founders' Bible
compiled by David Barton

Freedom Tide
by Chad Connelly

BOOKS CONT.

Original Intent
by David Barton

Pilgrims and Patriots
by Eddie L. Hyatt

A Republic If You Can Keep It
by Gai M. Ferdon, Ph.D.

Renewing the Soul of America
by Charles Crismer

Stealing the Minds of America
by Janice L. Ponds

Webster's 1828 American Dictionary of the English Language
by Noah Webster

What Were They Thinking?
by Carol Sewell

When Nations Die
by Jim Nelson Black

ABOUT THE AUTHOR

Dave Meyer is the vice president of *Joyce Meyer Ministries*. He has served in full-time ministry for more than 30 years, and his wisdom and stewardship in finance and administration have helped build *Joyce Meyer Ministries* into what it is today.

Dave has long been a stabilizing force behind the scenes, helping to support Joyce and build an organization that ministers the love and message of the Gospel to millions each year. His steadfastness, patience and obedience in waiting to hear God's voice are a cornerstone of this ministry.

A veteran of the United States Army, Dave is also passionate about America's Godly heritage and the history behind this nation's biblical principles. His heart is to pray for America and provide a spark that will encourage more Christians to pray, stand up for righteousness and exercise their right to vote.

Dave has been married to Joyce for over 50 years, and they have four grown children, 12 grandchildren and two great-grandchildren. Dave and Joyce Meyer make their home in St. Louis, Missouri.